Anonymus

Messrs. Bagster's Catalogue of Biblical and Miscellaneous Works

Anonymus

Messrs. Bagster's Catalogue of Biblical and Miscellaneous Works

ISBN/EAN: 9783741163586

Manufactured in Europe, USA, Canada, Australia, Japa

Cover: Foto ©Thomas Meinert / pixelio.de

Manufactured and distributed by brebook publishing software
(www.brebook.com)

Anonymus

Messrs. Bagster's Catalogue of Biblical and Miscellaneous Works

Messrs. BAGSTER'S

CATALOGUE

OF

BIBLICAL

AND

MISCELLANEOUS WORKS.

LONDON:

15, PATERNOSTER ROW.

1874.

TABLE OF CONTENTS.

ALPHABETICAL INDEX.

ℬ

SAMUEL BAGSTER AND SONS.

BIBLIA SACRA POLYGLOTTA.

THE MODERN POLYGLOT BIBLE

IN EIGHT LANGUAGES.

TWO VOLUMES, FOLIO.

	£	s.	d.
(N.B.) Issued in 12 parts, in stiff wrapper, .. each	0	10	6

The BIBLIA SACRA POLYGLOTTA is invaluable to the Biblical Student, who can, by its aid, compare with facility the various Texts of the Bible. Every Clergyman also, will find it a great addition to his library.

The advantages offered by this Polyglot Bible are great. Unlike the older Polyglots, it addresses itself primarily to the Interpretation of Scripture. It gives under one simultaneous view the Hebrew Text, the two ancient indispensable versions, the Septuagint and the Vulgate, and a series of the best European translations.

The older Polyglots, the Complutensian, the Antwerp, the Paris, and the London, are inaccessible to most people, and many would find a difficulty in using them; but this Modern Polyglot is at once accessible, convenient, moderate in price, and of easy practical use. The study of Hebrew is spreading every day, the Greek is familiar to most Biblical Students, while the Latin and European Versions are more or less universally understood.

Bishop Coverdale says in the prologue of his Bible, "Sure I am that there cometh more knowledge and understanding of the Scripture by their sundry translations, than by all the glosses of our sophistical doctors."

For Specimen Pages, see the Illustrated Supplement. By post, free.

2

	£	s.	d.

The New Testament is presented on a precisely
similar plan, with a Supplement containing the Peschito
Syriac Version.

This Polyglot also contains Tables of the Various
Readings of the Hebrew, the Septuagint, the Greek,
and Syriac New Testaments.

The Work is handsomely printed in Two Volumes,
Crown folio, and is issued ready bound in best morocco
Roxburgh 8 8 0

In Turkey morocco plain 11 11 0

 „ „ „ antique, hand-tooled edges,
for presentation 16 16 0

Also in 12 parts, stiff wrapper .. .. .. each 0 10 6

Or, Bound in Cloth. Two Volumes 6 6 0

Hic Liber continet :—Prolegomena in Biblia Polyglotta; Biblia Hebraica, ex editione celeberrima Ever-
ardi Van der Hooght, quæ a. d. 1705 lucem vidit, punctis
vocalibus et accentibus instructa; Versionem Græcam
Septuaginta Seniorum, juxta exemplar Vaticanum, a
Cardinali Carafa in lucem emissum ; Novum Testamen-
tum Græcum juxta textum, ut aiunt, Receptum ; Biblia
Sacra Vulgatæ Editionis Sixti V. et Clementis VIII.
jussu recognita atque edita ; Versionem Anglicanam,
lectionibus marginalibus, numerisque loca parallela
indicantibus adornatam; Versionem Germanicam a
Martino Luthero; Versionem Gallicam a Johanne
Frederico Ostervald; Versionem Italianam a Giovanni
Diodati ; Versionem Hispanicam a Patre Scio ; Novum
Testamentum Hebraicum a Gulielmo Greenfield ; et in
Appendice,—Syrorum Novi Testamenti Versionem, quam
Peschito nuncupant, juxta exemplar Viennense a Johanne
Alberto Widmanstadio, a. d. 1555 typis mandatum,
literis Syriacis atque punctis vocalibus instructam, cum-
que collatione editionis quam Societas ad Biblia Sacra
evulganda instituta in lucem emisit; Pentateuchum
Hebræo-Samaritanum juxta Kennicotti editionem ;
Varias Lectiones in Versionem LXX. ex editione Grabii;
Lectionis Varietates in Novum Testamentum Græcum,
e notis Griesbachii ductas.

For Specimen Pages, see the Illustrated Supplement. By post, free.

The Polyglot Bible Cabinet.　　　　　　　　　| £ *s. d.*

An elegantly Carved Oak Case, containing the
Hebrew, Greek, Latin, English, French, German,
Spanish, and Portuguese Bibles, the Syriac New
Testament, the Treasury of Scripture Parallels, with
Hebrew, Greek, and Syriac Lexicons, and Greek
and English Concordances. Eleven Volumes, bound
uniformly in "Bagster's flexible turkey morocco,"
tooled　..　　..　　..　　..　　..　　..　　..　　..　15　15　0

For Specimen Pages, see the Illustrated Supplement. By post, free.

11 And *that* every tongue should confess that Jesus Christ is Lord,[a] to the glory of God the Father.

12 Wherefore, my beloved, as ye have always obeyed, not as in my presence only, but now much more in my absence, work[b] out your own salvation with fear and trembling:

13 For it is God[c] which worketh in you both to will and to do of *his* good pleasure.

14 Do all things without murmurings and disputings:[d]

15 That ye may be blameless and harmless,[e] the sons[f] of God, without

A. D. 64.

a John 13. 13.
Ro. 14. 9.
b Ac. 12. 6
c Ac. 20. 24.
Ga. 1. 15, 16.
d 1 Ti. 10. 16.
Jno 6. 37. 38
He. 4. 11.
e Pe. 1. 3. 16.
f Ep. 4. 1.
f La. 1. 4.
g He. 13. 21.
g Is. 52. 11.

that he hath whereof he might trust : *if* the flesh, I more:

5 Circumcised the eighth day, of the stock of Israel, of the tribe of Benjamin, an Hebrew of the Hebrews; as touching the law, a Pharisee;[g]

6 Concerning zeal,[c] persecuting the church; touching the righteousness which is in the law, blameless.

7 But what things were gain to me, those I counted loss[f] for Christ.

8 Yea, doubtless, and I count all things *but* loss, for[c] the excellency of the knowledge of Christ Jesus my Lord: for whom I have[g] suffered the loss of all things, and do count them *but* dung, that I may

---

II.

Practical religion.   PHILIPPIANS, III.   *Confidence in Christ alone.*

11 And *that* every tongue should confess that Jesus Christ is Lord,[a] to the glory of God the Father.

12 Wherefore, my beloved, as ye have always obeyed, not as in my presence only, but now much more in my absence, work[b] out your own salvation with fear

BAGSTER'S POLYGLOT BIBLES.

ENGLISH VERSION.

THE FACSIMILE SERIES.

I. The MINIATURE Edition.
II. The MEDIUM Edition.
III. The LARGE TYPE Edition.

These Editions correspond page for page, and line
for line, and thus secure for the reader the great advantage pointed out by Dr. Watts: "It has been some
advantage for this reason to accustom one's self to books
of the same Edition; and it has been of constant and
special use to Divines and private Christians, to be
furnished with several Bibles of the same Edition, that,
wheresoever they are, whether in their chamber, parlour,
or study, in the younger or elder years of life, they may
find the chapters and verses standing in the same parts
of the page."

(I.) The Miniature Polyglot Bible.   16mo.

With a complete Index of Subjects.

CONTENTS:—The Authorised Version of the Old and
New Testaments, with the following supplementary
illustrative matters.—Preface; a detailed Chronological
Arrangement of the Old Testament Scriptures; Tables
of Measures, Weights, and Coins; an Itinerary of the
Children of Israel from Egypt to Canaan; Table of
the Chronological Order of the Books of the Bible;
Chronological Table of the Kings and Prophets of Judah
and Israel, in Parallel Columns; a Summary View of
the principal events of the period from the close of the
sacred Canon of the Old Testament; an Account of the
Jewish and other Sects and Factions; a Table of the
principal Messianic Prophecies; a List of Passages in

For Specimen Pages, see page 4.

the Old Testament quoted or alluded to in the New
Testament; the Names, Titles, and Characters of our
Lord Jesus Christ; a Chronological Harmony of the
Four Evangelists, in Parallel Columns; a Scripture Text-
book; a series of Coloured Maps, and an engraved
Chronological Chart of History from B.C. 500 to A.D. 400;
and an Alphabetical Index to the Psalms.

			£	s.	d.
Seconds morocco blocked, gilt edges			0	9	0
Turkey morocco plain			0	11	6
„ „ hand tooled			0	15	0
„ „ plain antique, red under gold edges			0	17	0
„ „ or russia, antique, tooled edges, etc.			1	2	0
„ „ limp, with flaps			0	17	6
„ „ lined calf, with protecting edges and elastic band			1	0	0
One best treble-gilt clasp			0	4	0
Silver clasps to order.					
Black roan reading cover, with flaps over the leaves			0	1	0
Turkey morocco ditto ditto ..			0	4	6
A set of 25 Photographs, extra			0	7	6

(II.) The Medium Polyglot Bible.   *Foolscap octavo.*

With a complete Index of Subjects.

These Editions correspond page for page, and line
for line, and thus secure for the reader the great advantage pointed out by Dr. Watts: "It has been some
advantage for this reason to accustom one's self to books
of the same Edition: and it has been of constant and
special use to Divines and private Christians, to be
furnished with several Bibles of the same Edition, that,
wheresoever they are, whether in their chamber, parlour, or study, in the younger or elder years of life,
they may find the chapters and verses standing in the
same parts of the page."

CONTENTS:—The Authorised Version of the Old
and New Testaments, with the following supplementary
illustrative matters.—Preface; a detailed Chronological
Arrangement of the Old Testament Scriptures; Tables

For Specimen Pages, see page 4.

	£	s.	d.

of Measures, Weights, and Coins; an Itinerary of the
Children of Israel from Egypt to Canaan; Table of the
Chronological Order of the Books of the Bible; Chronological Table of the Kings and Prophets of Judah and
Israel, in Parallel Columns; a Summary View of the
principal events of the period from the close of the Sacred
Canon of the Old Testament, until the times of the New
Testament; an Account of the Jewish and other Sects
and Factions; a Table of the principal Messianic Prophecies; a List of Passages in the Old Testament quoted
or alluded to in the New Testament; the Names, Titles,
and Characters of our Lord Jesus Christ; a Chronological Harmony of the Four Evangelists, in Parallel
Columns; a Scripture Text-book; a series of Coloured
Maps, and an engraved Chronological Chart of History
from B.C. 500 to A.D. 400; and an Alphabetical Index
to the Psalms.

			£	s.	d.
Seconds morocco blocked, gilt edges			0	12	0
Turkey morocco plain, stiff or limp covers ..			0	16	6
„ „ hand-tooled, stiff or limp covers			1	0	0
„ „ limp, with flaps			1	2	6
„ „ plain antique, red under gold edges			1	2	0
„ „ or russia antique, tooled edges			1	0	6
„ „ limp, lined calf, with protecting edges and elastic band			1	5	0
One best treble-gilt clasp			0	5	0
Silver clasps to order.					
Black roan reading covers, with flaps over the leaves			0	2	6
Turkey morocco ditto ditto			0	5	6

(III.) The Large-Type Polyglot Bible. *Octavo.*

With a complete Index of Subjects.

These Editions correspond page for page, and line
for line, and thus secure for the reader the great advantage pointed out by Dr. Watts: "It has been some

For Specimen Pages, see page 1.

advantage for this reason to accustom one's self to books of the same Edition: and it has been of constant and special use to Divines and private Christians, to be furnished with several Bibles of the same Edition, that, wheresoever they are, whether in their chamber, parlour, or study, in the younger or older years of life, they may find the chapters and verses standing in the same parts of the page.

CONTENTS:—The Authorised Version of the Old and New Testaments, with the following supplementary illustrative matters.—Preface; a detailed Chronological Arrangement of the Old Testament Scriptures; Tables of Measures, Weights, and Coins; an Itinerary of the Children of Israel from Egypt to Canaan; Table of the Chronological Order of the Books of the Bible; Chronological Table of the Kings and Prophets of Judah and Israel, in Parallel Columns; a Summary View of the principal events of the period from the close of the Sacred Canon of the Old Testament, until the times of the New Testament; an Account of the Jewish and other Sects and Factions; a Table of the principal Messianic prophecies; a List of Passages in the Old Testament quoted or alluded to in the New Testament; the Names, Titles, and Characters of our Lord Jesus Christ; a Chronological Harmony of the Four Evangelists, in Parallel Columns; a Scripture Text-book; a series of Coloured Maps, and an engraved Chronological Chart of History from B.C. 500 to A.D. 400; and an Alphabetical Index to the Psalms.

			£	s.	d.
Seconds, morocco, blocked, gilt edges	..	..	0	14	0
Turkey morocco plain, stiff or limp covers	..		1	1	0
„	„	hand tooled, stiff or limp covers	1	5	0
„	„	limp with flaps	1	7	6
„	„	plain antique, red under gold edges	1	7	0
„	„	or russia, antique, with bevelled boards, tooled leaves	1	18	0

For Specimen Pages, see page 4.

	£	s.	d.
Turkey morocco limp, lined calf, protecting edges, and elastic band　.. 　..	1	10	0
One best treble-gilt clasp　.. 　.. 　.. 　..	0	3	6
Silver clasps to order.			
Black roan reading covers, with flaps over the leaves 　.. 　..	0	3	0
Turkey morocco　ditto　ditto .. 　.. 　..	0	8	0

An Edition of No. III, page 7, printed upon Royal
　　　· octavo writing-paper.

	£	s.	d.
Cloth　.. 　.. 　.. 　.. 　.. 　..	1	1	0
Turkey morocco plain .. 　.. 　.. 　..	1	15	0

BAGSTER'S POLYGLOT BIBLES.

THE FACSIMILE SERIES: { No. I., The MINIATURE Edition, 16mo.
No. II., The MEDIUM Edition, Foolscap octavo.
No. III., The LARGE PRINT Edition, Octavo.

THESE three Editions correspond page for page, and line for line, to afford to those who use more than one Edition of the Series the inestimable help of local memory. "It has been some advantage for this reason to accustom one's self to books of the same Edition : and it has been of constant and special use to Divines and private Christians, to be furnished with several Bibles of the same Edition, that, whensoever they are, whether in their chamber, parlour, or study, in the younger or elder years of life, they may find the chapters and verses standing in the same parts of the page."—*Art of Improving the Memory.*

BAGSTER'S POLYGLOT BIBLES.

These Bibles are enriched with the following supplementary aids:—A detailed Chronological Arrangement of the Old Testament Scriptures; Tables of Measures, Weights, and Coins; an Itinerary of the Children of Israel from Egypt to Canaan; Table of the Chronological Order of the Books of the Bible; Chronological Table of the Kings and Prophets of Judah and Israel, in Parallel Columns; a Summary View of the principal events of the period from the close of the sacred Canon of the Old Testament, until the times of the New Testament; an Account of the Jewish and other Sects and Factions; a Table of the principal Messianic Prophecies; a List of Passages in the Old Testament quoted or alluded to in the New Testament; the Names, Titles, and Characters of our Lord Jesus Christ; a Chronological Harmony of the Four Evangelists, in Parallel Columns; Coloured Maps; an engraved Chronological Chart of History from B.C. 500 to A.D. 400; a condensed Scripture Index; and an Alphabetical Index to the Psalms.

Another not unimportant advantage is secured by printing these Bibles on the facsimile principle; they not only correspond one with another, but with the whole Polyglot series of Hebrew, Greek, Latin, German, and other languages, which are all arranged on the same convenient plan. See Index, under Polyglot Bibles.

	Roan or cloth, blocked, gilt edges	Turkey cover, jointed	Persian morocco, hard boards	Antique mor., loaded, gold on red edges	Plain antique morocco, plain gold on red edges	Limp Turkey morocco, with protecting flaps	Levant mor., lined calf, extra perfectly supple.
I. The Miniature Polyglot Bible, 16mo.	0 9	0 0 12	6 0 15	0 1 2	0 0 17	0 0 17	6 1 0 0
Do. with the Book of Common Prayer	0 11	0 0 14	6 0 17	0 1 4	0 0 19	0 0 19	6 1 2 0
Do. with the Psalms of the Church of Scotland	0 9	6 0 13	0 0 15	6 0 15	2	6 0 18	6 0 18	0 1 0 6
Do. with Wesley's Hymns	0 13	6 0 17	6 1 0	0 1	0 7	0 1 2	0 2	6 1 0 5 0
Do. with Greek and English Test.	0 14	0 0 18	6 1 1	0 1	0 7	0 1 2	0 5	0 1 5 0
Do. with 108 Pictorial Illustrations	0 17	0 1 0	6 1 3	0 10	0 1 5	0 1 5	0 1 8 0
II. The Medium Polyglot Bible. Fcp. 8vo.	0 12	0 0 16	6 1 1	0 0 1	6 1 6	0 1 2	2	6 2 6 1	5 0
Do. with the Book of Common Prayer	0 14	0 0 18	6 1 2	0 6	6 1 4	0 4	6 1 4	6 1 7 0
Do. with the Apocrypha	0 14	0 0 18	6 1 1	5	6 1 4	0 4	6 1 4	6 1 7 0
Do. with Cruden's Concordance	0 16	0 1 0	6 1 4	8	6 1 6	0 6	6 1 6	6 1 9 0
III. The Medium, Psalms of the Church of Scotland	0 12	6 0 17	0 1 0	0 7	0 1 2	0 3	0 6 1 5 6
Do. with Wesley's Hymns	0 18	0 1 2	6 1 6	12	6 1 8	0 8	6 1 6 1	0 1 11 0
Do. with Greek and English New Test.	0 17	0 1 1	6 1 5	11	6 1 7	0 7	6 1 6	0 1 10 0
Do. with 108 Pictorial Illustrations	1 0	0 1 4	6 1 8	14	6 1 10	0 10	6 1 13	0 1 13 0
III. The Large-print Polyglot Bible. 8vo.	0 14	0 1 1	0 1 5	18	0 1 7	0 7	0 1 10	0 1 10 0
Do. with the Book of Common Prayer	0 16	6 1 3	6 1 7	0	6 1 9	6 1 9	0 1 10	6 1 12 6
Do. with the Apocrypha	0 17	0 1 4	0 1 8	1	0 1 10	0 1 10	6 1 13	0 1 13 0
III. The Large-print, Psalms of the Church of Scotland	0 15	0 1 2	0 1 6	19	0 1 8	0 1 8	6 1 11	0 1 11 0
Do. with Greek and English Test.	1 0	6 1 7	6 1 11	6 2 4	6 1 13	6 1 14	0 1 16	6 1 16 6
Do. with Cruden's Concordance	0 18	6 1 5	6 1 9	6 2 2	6 1 11	6 1 12	0 1 14	6 1 14 6

*** The Book of Common Prayer, the Scripture Index, the Psalms of the Church of Scotland, the Apocrypha, etc., may be bound up with these Bibles in any desired combination.

POLYGLOT BIBLES, Etc..

HEBREW.

	£ s. d.
The Hebrew Bible of the Polyglot Series.	
CONTENTS:—The Hebrew Text after Van der Hooght, with the *Keri* and *Chetib*, 8×5 pp. The Various Readings of the Samaritan Pentateuch, 50 pp.	
Foolscap octavo, Cloth	0 10 0
Hebrew and English Old Testament, interpaged.	
Foolscap octavo, Cloth	0 18 0
With GREEK and ENGLISH NEW TESTAMENT. extra	0 6 0
Hebrew Bible, interpaged with the Greek Septuagint.	
Foolscap octavo, Cloth	1 0 0
Hebrew and Latin Vulgate Old Testament, interpaged.	
Foolscap octavo, Cloth	0 14 6
Hebrew and German Old Testament, interpaged.	
Foolscap octavo, Cloth	0 14 6
Hebrew and French Old Testament, interpaged.	
Foolscap octavo, Cloth	0 14 6
Hebrew and Italian Old Testament, interpaged.	
Foolscap octavo, Cloth	0 14 6
Hebrew and Spanish Old Testament, interpaged.	
Foolscap octavo, Cloth	0 14 6
Hebrew and Portuguese Old Testament, interpaged.	
Foolscap octavo, Cloth	0 14 6
Hebrew Version of the New Testament.	
Octavo Cloth	0 6 0
Hebrew Version of the New Testament.	
Foolscap octavo, Cloth	0 3 6
Hebrew Version of the New Testament.	
32mo. Cloth	0 3 6

GREEK.

The Septuagint, interpaged with the Hebrew Text.	
Foolscap octavo, Cloth	1 0 0

For Specimen Pages, see the Illustrated Supplement. By post, free.

	£.	s.	d.
Greek Septuagint and English Old Testament, interpaged.			
Foolscap octavo, Cloth	0	18	0
With GREEK and ENGLISH NEW TESTAMENT, each	0	6	0
Greek and Latin Bible, interpaged.			
Foolscap octavo, Cloth	1	0	6
Greek and German Bible, interpaged.			
Foolscap octavo, Cloth	1	0	6
Greek and French Bible, interpaged.			
Foolscap octavo, Cloth	1	0	6
Greek and Italian Bible, interpaged.			
Foolscap octavo, Cloth	1	0	6
Greek and Spanish Bible, interpaged.			
Foolscap octavo, Cloth	1	0	6
Greek and Portuguese Bible, interpaged.			
Foolscap octavo, Cloth	1	0	6
Greek New Testament, large print.			
Octavo, Cloth	0	12	0
Greek New Testament.			
Foolscap octavo, Cloth	0	3	6
Greek New Testament. *Narrow Edition.*			
32mo.	0	4	6
Greek New Testament. *Polymicrian Edition.*			
32mo., Cloth	0	3	6
Greek Common Prayer.			
Foolscap octavo, Cloth	0	2	6
Greek Common Prayer. *Polymicrian Edition.*			
32mo., Cloth	0	2	6
Modern Greek Common Prayer.			
Foolscap octavo, Cloth	0	2	6
Modern Greek Common Prayer. *Polymicrian Edition.*			
32 mo., Cloth	0	2	6
Greek Psalter. (Ancient and Modern.)			
32mo., Roan, gilt edges .. .. .. each	0	1	0

For Specimen Pages, see the Illustrated Supplement. By post free.

ENGLISH.

English and Hebrew Old Testament, interpaged.

	£	s.	d.
Foolscap octavo, Cloth	0	18	0
English and Greek New Testament, extra	0	6	0

English and Greek Septuagint, interpaged.

| Foolscap octavo, Cloth | 0 | 18 | 0 |
| English and Greek New Testament, extra | 0 | 6 | 0 |

English and Latin Bible, interpaged.

| Foolscap octavo, Cloth | 0 | 17 | 6 |

English and German Bible, interpaged.

| Foolscap octavo, Cloth | 0 | 17 | 6 |

English and French Bible, interpaged.

| Foolscap octavo, Cloth | 0 | 17 | 6 |

English and Italian Bible, interpaged.

| Foolscap octavo, Cloth | 0 | 17 | 6 |

English and Spanish Bible, interpaged.

| Foolscap octavo, Cloth | 0 | 17 | 6 |

English and Portuguese Bible, interpaged.

| Foolscap octavo, Cloth | 0 | 17 | 6 |

English New Testament. *Thin Edition.*

| Octavo, Limp morocco | 0 | 10 | 0 |

English New Testament. *Thin Edition.*

| Foolscap octavo, Limp morocco | 0 | 6 | 6 |

English New Testament.

| 16mo., Limp morocco | 0 | 5 | 6 |

English New Testament. *Narrow Edition.*

| 32mo. Roan | 0 | 6 | 0 |

English New Testament. *Polymicrian Edition.*

| 32mo., Cloth | 0 | 2 | 6 |
| Turkey morocco plain | 0 | 6 | 0 |

English Psalter.

| 32mo. Roan, gilt edges | 0 | 1 | 0 |

For Specimen Pages, see the Illustrated Supplement. By post, free.

LATIN.

Latin Bible, of the Pocket Polyglot Series.

£ s. d.

CONTENTS:— Biblia Sacra Vulgatæ Editionis Sixti V. et Clementis VIII. jussu recognita atque edita, 773 pp.

Foolscap octavo, Cloth 0 7 0

Turkey morocco plain 0 15 0

Latin and Hebrew Old Testament, interpaged.

Foolscap octavo, Cloth 0 14 6

Latin and Greek Bible, interpaged.

Foolscap octavo, Cloth 1 0 6

Latin and English Bible, interpaged.

Foolscap octavo, Cloth 0 17 6

Latin and German Bible, interpaged.

Foolscap octavo, Cloth 0 14 0

Latin and French Bible, interpaged.

Foolscap octavo, Cloth 0 14 0

Latin and Italian Bible, interpaged.

Foolscap octavo, Cloth 0 14 0

Latin and Spanish Bible, interpaged.

Foolscap octavo, Cloth 0 14 0

Latin and Portuguese Bible, interpaged.

Foolscap octavo, Cloth 0 14 0

Latin New Testament.

Foolscap octavo, Cloth 0 2 6

Latin New Testament, *Polymicrian Edition.*

32mo., Cloth 0 2 6

Turkey morocco plain 0 6 0

Latin Common Prayer.

Foolscap octavo, Cloth 0 2 6

Latin Common Prayer. *Polymicrian Edition.*

32mo. Cloth 0 2 6

Turkey morocco plain 0 6 0

Latin Psalter.

32mo Roan, gilt edges 0 1 0

GERMAN.

	£ s. d.
German Bible, of the Pocket Polyglot Series.	
Martin Luther's Version of the Old and New Testaments, 773 pp.	
Foolscap octavo, Cloth	0 7 0
Turkey morocco plain	0 15 0
German and Hebrew Old Testament, interpaged.	
Foolscap octavo, Cloth	0 14 6
German and Greek Bible, interpaged.	
Foolscap octavo, Cloth	1 0 6
German and English Bible, interpaged.	
Foolscap octavo, Cloth	0 17 6
German and Latin Bible, interpaged.	
Foolscap octavo, Cloth	0 14 0
German and French Bible, interpaged.	
Foolscap octavo, Cloth	0 14 0
German and Italian Bible, interpaged.	
Foolscap octavo, Cloth	0 14 0
German and Spanish Bible, interpaged.	
Foolscap, octavo, Cloth	0 14 0
German and Portuguese Bible, interpaged.	
Foolscap octavo, Cloth	0 14 0
German New Testament.	
Foolscap octavo, Cloth	0 2 6
German New Testament. *Polymicrian Edition.*	
32mo., Cloth	0 2 6
Turkey morocco plain	0 6 0
German Common Prayer.	
Foolscap octavo, Cloth	0 2 6
German Common Prayer. *Polymicrian Edition.*	
32mo., Cloth	0 2 6
Turkey morocco plain	0 6 0
German Psalter.	
32mo. Roan, gilt edges	0 1 0

FRENCH.

	£	s.	d.
French Bible, of the Pocket Polyglot Series.			
By Ostervald, 773 pp.			
Foolscap octavo, Cloth	0	7	0
Turkey morocco plain	0	15	0
French and Hebrew Old Testament, interpaged.			
Foolscap octavo, Cloth	0	14	6
French and Greek Bible, interpaged.			
Foolscap octavo, Cloth	1	0	6
French and English Bible, interpaged.			
Foolscap octavo, Cloth	0	17	6
French and Latin Bible, interpaged.			
Foolscap octavo, Cloth	0	14	0
French and German Bible, interpaged.			
Foolscap octavo, Cloth	0	14	0
French and Italian Bible, interpaged.			
Foolscap octavo, Cloth	0	14	0
French and Spanish Bible, interpaged.			
Foolscap octavo, Cloth	0	14	0
French and Portuguese Bible, interpaged.			
Foolscap octavo, Cloth	0	14	0
Miniature French Bible. (Martin's Version.)			
18mo., Cloth	0	7	0
Turkey morocco plain	0	13	6
Miniature French and English Bible, interpaged.			
18mo., Cloth	0	12	0
Turkey morocco plain	0	18	0
French New Testament.			
Foolscap octavo, Cloth	0	2	6
French New Testament. *Polymicrian Edition.*			
32mo., Cloth	0	2	6
Turkey morocco plain	0	6	0
French Common Prayer.			
Octavo, Cloth	0	7	0
French Common Prayer.			
Foolscap octavo, Cloth	0	2	6
French Common Prayer. *Polymicrian Edition.*			
32mo., Cloth	0	2	6
Turkey morocco plain	0	6	0
French Psalter.			
32mo., Roan; gilt edges...	0	1	0

For Specimen Pages, see the Illustrated Supplement. By post, free.

3

ITALIAN.

	£	s.	d.
Italian Bible, of the Pocket Polyglot Series.			
By Giovanni Diodati, 773 pp.			
Foolscap octavo, Cloth	0	7	0
Turkey morocco plain	0	15	0
Italian and Hebrew Old Testament, interpaged.			
Foolscap octavo, Cloth	0	14	6
Italian and Greek Bible, interpaged.			
Foolscap octavo, Cloth	1	0	6
Italian and English Bible, interpaged.			
Foolscap octavo, Cloth	0	17	6
Italian and Latin Bible, interpaged.			
Foolscap octavo, Cloth	0	14	0
Italian and French Bible, interpaged.			
Foolscap octavo, Cloth	0	14	0
Italian and German Bible, interpaged.			
Foolscap octavo, Cloth	0	14	0
Italian and Spanish Bible, interpaged.			
Foolscap octavo, Cloth	0	14	0
Italian and Portuguese Bible, interpaged.			
Foolscap octavo, Cloth	0	14	0
Italian New Testament.			
Foolscap octavo, Cloth	0	2	6
Italian New Testament. *Polymicrian Edition.*			
32mo., Cloth	0	2	6
Turkey morocco plain	0	6	0
Italian Common Prayer.			
Foolscap octavo, Cloth	0	2	6
Italian Common Prayer. *Polymicrian Edition.*			
32mo., Cloth	0	2	6
Turkey morocco plain	0	6	0
Italian Psalter.			
32mo., Roan, gilt edges...	0	1	0

For Specimen Pages, see the Illustrated Supplement. By post, free.

SPANISH.

	£	s.	d.
Spanish Bible, of the Pocket Polyglot Series.			

CONTENTS:—La Biblià ó el Antiguo y Nuevo Testamento, traducidos en Español por el Rmo. P. Phelipe Scio de S. Miguel, 773 pp.

	£	s.	d.
Foolscap octavo, Cloth	0	7	0
Turkey morocco plain	0	15	0
Spanish and Hebrew Old Testament, interpaged.			
Foolscap octavo, Cloth	0	14	6
Spanish and Latin Bible, interpaged.			
Foolscap octavo, Cloth	0	14	0
Spanish and Greek Bible, interpaged.			
Foolscap octavo, Cloth	1	0	6
Spanish and English Bible, interpaged			
Foolscap octavo, Cloth	0	17	6
Spanish and French Bible, interpaged.			
Foolscap octavo, Cloth	0	14	0
Spanish and Italian Bible interpaged.			
Foolscap octavo, Cloth	0	14	0
Spanish and German Bible, interpaged.			
Foolscap octavo, Cloth	0	14	0
Spanish and Portuguese Bible, interpaged.			
Foolscap octavo, Cloth	0	14	0
Spanish New Testament.			
Foolscap octavo, Cloth	0	1	6
Spanish New Testament. *Polymierian Edition.*			
32mo., Cloth	0	1	6
Turkey morocco plain	0	6	0
Spanish Common Prayer.			
Foolscap octavo, Cloth	0	1	6
Spanish Common Prayer *Polymierian Edition.*			
32mo., Cloth	0	1	6
Turkey morocco plain	0	6	0
Spanish Psalter.			
32mo., Roan, gilt edges	0	1	0

For Specimen Pages, see the Illustrated Supplement. By post, free.

PORTUGUESE.

Portuguese Bible, of the Pocket Polyglot Series.

£ *s. d.*

CONTENTS :—A Santa Biblia contendo o Velho e o
Novo Testamento, traduzido em Portuguez segundo a
Vulgata.

Foolscap octavo, Cloth	0	7	0
Turkey morocco plain	0	15	0

Portuguese and Hebrew Old Testament, interpaged.

Foolscap octavo, Cloth .. .. | 0 | 14 | 6 |

Portuguese and Greek Bible, interpaged.

Foolscap octavo, Cloth .. .. | 1 | 0 | 6 |

Portuguese and English Bible, interpaged.

Foolscap octavo, Cloth .. .. | 0 | 17 | 6 |

Portuguese and Latin Bible, interpaged.

Foolscap octavo, Cloth .. .. .. | 0 | 14 | 0 |

Portuguese and French Bible, interpaged.

Foolscap octavo, Cloth .. .. | 0 | 14 | 0 |

Portuguese and Italian Bible, interpaged.

Foolscap octavo, Cloth .. .. | 0 | 14 | 0 |

Portuguese and Spanish Bible, interpaged.

Foolscap octavo, Cloth .. .. .. | 0 | 14 | 0 |

Portuguese and German Bible, interpaged.

Foolscap octavo, Cloth .. .. .. | 0 | 14 | 0 |

Portuguese New Testament.

Foolscap octavo, Cloth .. .. | 0 | 3 | 6 |

For Specimen Pages, see the Illustrated Supplement. By post, free.

THE COMPREHENSIVE BIBLE.

CROWN QUARTO.

The Comprehensive Bible, in Small Pica Type.

The TEXT is the Authorised Version printed in a bold readable type, illustrated with more than half a million of References, selected and arranged; with very numerous Notes, Critical, Geographical, Historical, and explanatory; with Introductory and Concluding Remarks upon each Book, etc.

The INTRODUCTION to the Work contains a Summary of the Evidences of the Genuineness, Uncorrupted Preservation, Authenticity, and Inspiration of the Sacred Writings:—an Account of the Divisions and Marks of Distinction which occur in the Scriptures:—of the Manuscripts and early printed editions of the Scriptures:—of the Samaritan Pentateuch, Ancient Versions, and also the Authorised English Version:—of the Jewish Writings, the Apostolic and Primitive Fathers, and the Doctors of the Church:—of the Jewish Sects, Factions, and Orders of Men, mentioned in the Scriptures:—of the Jewish and other Measures, Weights, and Coins:—of the Jewish and Roman Modes of computing Time:—an Outline of the Geography and History of the Nations mentioned in the Scriptures.

With the PREFACE there are included the Translators' Dedication to King James:—the Translators' Preface to the Reader:—the Names and Order of the Books of the Old and New Testaments:—the Chronological Order of the Sacred Books, with the Abbreviations used in this Work:—a Chronological Arrangement of the Old and New Testaments.

The SUPPLEMENTARY matter includes a History of the Period from the close of the Canon of the Old Testament until the Times of the New Testament:—a Harmony of the Four Gospels:—a General Index:—and a Family Register.

	£	s.	d.
With SCOTCH PSALMS, extra	0	1	0
With APOCRYPHA, extra	0	4	0
With RED BORDERS, extra	0	6	0
Cloth (Half-morocco to order.)	1	10	0
Turkey morocco plain	1	6	0
,, ,, or russia, hand-tooled	2	15	0
Levant morocco, plain antique, red under gold edges	3	0	0
Richly-tooled edges, extra	0	5	0
Levant morocco or russia, antique, tooled edges, bevelled boards, etc., etc.	3	12	6
One treble-gilt clasp, from	1	1	0
One ditto clasp and corners	1	5	0
Treble-gilt inscription plates, from	0	15	0
Soft leather reading covers, with flaps over the leaves, in black roan	0	9	0
Cases in oak, velvet linings, lock and key	1	11	6

For Specimen Pages, see the Illustrated Supplement. By post, free.

THE COMPREHENSIVE BIBLE.

MEDIUM QUARTO.

	£	s.	d.
The Comprehensive Bible, in Pica Type.			
CONTENTS :—(See page 21.)			
With APOCRYPHA, extra	0	4	0
With CRUDEN's CONCORDANCE, extra	0	5	0
With SCOTCH PSALMS, extra	0	2	0
Cloth (Half-morocco to order.)	1	15	0
Turkey morocco plain, gilt leaves	2	15	0
„ „ or russia, hand-tooled	3	5	0
„ „ plain antique, red under gold edges	3	10	0
Richly-tooled edges, extra	0	5	0
Levant morocco or russia, antique, tooled edges, bevelled boards, etc., etc.	4	5	0
One treble-gilt clasp, 2 inches wide, from	1	3	6
One clasp and corners, treble gilt	2	9	0
Treble-gilt inscription plates, from	0	17	6
Soft leather reading covers, with flaps over the leaves, in black roan	0	12	0
Cases in oak, velvet linings, lock and key.. ..	1	16	0
An Edition of the Comprehensive Bible printed on			
Super Royal writing-paper, with four inches of blank margin. Imperial quarto.			
Cloth (Half-bound morocco to order.)	2	2	0

For Specimen Pages, see the Illustrated Supplement. By post, free.

THE MINIATURE QUARTO BIBLE.

AN EDITION OF THE SCRIPTURES

PREPARED EXPRESSLY FOR THE USE OF THOSE

TO WHOM LIGHTNESS, LARGE TYPE, AND SUPERIOR FINISH

ARE RECOMMENDATIONS.

	£	s.	d.
The Miniature Quarto Bible.			
It is printed upon the finest toned paper, and contains copious Critical Notes, Parallel References, Coloured Maps, etc., etc.			
This elegant volume measures about 7in. by 9½., and is not more than 2½in. in thickness.			
With CRUDEN's CONCORDANCE, extra	0	5	0
With SCOTCH PSALMS, extra	0	2	0
Cloth (Half-morocco to order.)	1	4	0
Turkey morocco plain	1	14	0
„ „ or russia, hand-tooled	2	0	0
Levant morocco, plain antique, red under gold edges	2	2	0
Richly tooled edges, extra	0	4	0
Turkey morocco limp, with flaps	2	5	0
Levant morocco or russia, antique, tooled edges, bevelled boards, etc.	2	15	0
One treble-gilt clasp, from	0	12	0
Clasps and corners, treble-gilt	1	11	0
Treble-gilt inscription plates, from	0	10	6
Soft leather reading covers, with flaps over the leaves, in black roan	0	6	6
Cases in oak, velvet linings, lock and key.. ..	1	10	0
Four Volumes, Turkey morocco limp, "for invalids"	4	0	0

For Specimen Pages, see the Illustrated Supplement. By post, free.

THE INVALID'S BIBLE.

The Large-Print Paragraph Bible, in separate Books. | £ s. d.

Crown octavo.

	£	s.	d.
Twenty-nine Volumes, Cloth extra, red edges ..	2	14	0
Genesis, Cloth extra, red edges	0	2	0
Exodus	0	2	0
Leviticus	0	1	6
Numbers	0	2	0
Deuteronomy	0	2	0
Joshua	0	1	8
Judges and Ruth	0	1	8
I. and II. Samuel	0	2	6
I. and II. Kings	0	2	6
I. and II. Chronicles	0	2	6
Ezra, Nehemiah, Esther	0	1	8
Job	0	1	6
Psalms	0	2	6
Proverbs, Ecclesiastes, Song of Songs ..	0	2	0
Isaiah	0	2	6
Jeremiah and Lamentations	0	2	6
Ezekiel	0	2	0
Daniel to Malachi	0	2	6
Matthew	0	1	6
Mark	0	1	4
Luke	0	1	8
John	0	1	6
The Acts	0	1	8
Romans	0	1	4
I. and II. Corinthians	0	1	4
Galatians to Philemon	0	2	6
Hebrews	0	1	6
James to Jude	0	1	6
Revelation	0	1	4

This edition of the Scriptures is peculiarly suitable for Invalids.

The Large-Print Paragraph Bible. In Four Vols.

	£	s.	d.
Cloth extra, red edges	2	2	0
Turkey morocco, plain	3	3	0
Turkey morocco, limp	3	3	0
Vol. I., containing Genesis to Deuteronomy, cloth extra	0	8	0
Vol. II. „ Joshua to Job	0	14	0
Vol. III. „ Psalms to Malachi ..	0	11	0
Vol. IV. „ Matthew to Revelation	0	12	0

For Specimen Pages, see the Illustrated Supplement. By post, free.

THE COMMENTARY WHOLLY BIBLICAL.

CONTENTS :—The Commentary: an Exposition of the Old and New Testaments in the very words of Scripture. 2244 pp. II. An outline of the Geography and History of the Nations mentioned in Scripture. III. Tables of Measures, Weights, and Coins. IV. An Itinerary of the Children of Israel from Egypt to the Promised Land. V. A Chronological comparative Table of the Kings and Prophets of Israel and Judah. VI. A Chart of the World's History from Adam to the Third Century A.D. VII. A complete Series of illustrative Maps. IX. A Chronological Arrangement of the Old and New Testaments. X. An Index to Doctrines and Subjects, with numerous Selected Passages, quoted in full. XI. An Index to the Names of Persons mentioned in Scripture. XII. An Index to the Names of Places found in Scripture. XIII. The Names, Titles, and Characters of Jesus Christ our Lord, as revealed in the Scriptures, methodically arranged.

Three Volumes, Quarto.

							£	s.	d.
Cloth	..	..	..	..	..	..	3	16	0
Half-morocco or russia	..	..	..	..	..	3	9	0
Turkey morocco plain	..	..	..	..	..	4	19	0
„ „ tooled	..	..	..	..	..	5	11	0
„ „ antique, hand-tooled		..	..	7	4	0

For Specimen Pages, see the Illustrated Supplement. By post, free.

STUDENTS' BIBLES, AND BIBLES
FOR MS. NOTES.

	£	s.	d.

The Treasury of Scripture Knowledge.

CONTENTS:— A selection of more than 500,000 Scripture References and Parallel Passages, methodically arranged to suit all editions of the Holy Scriptures. With numerous illustrative Notes; a Harmony of the Four Evangelists, Chronologically arranged; and a copious Alphabetical Index, 821 *pp.*

Foolscap octavo, Cloth	0	7	6
Turkey morocco plain	0	14	0
„ „ tooled	0	18	0

The Treasury Bible.

This is an edition of the above, interleaved with the Medium Polyglot Bible.

Foolscap octavo, Cloth	0	16	0
Turkey morocco plain	1	5	0
„ „ tooled	1	10	0

The Treasury Bible for MS. Notes.

CONTENTS:—The Authorised English Version, accompanied with a collection of about 500,000 selected Illustrative Passages, and numerous Critical Notes, 773 *pp.* Index of Subjects, 18 *pp.* This edition of the Scriptures is one of the series prepared for the reception of MS. Annotations. It is printed on fine writing-paper, in the fabric of which are waterlines, and one half of each page is left blank.

Quarto, Cloth	1	0	0

The Blank-paged Bible.

CONTENTS:—The Holy Scriptures of the Old and New Testaments, with copious References to Parallel and Illustrative Passages, and the alternate pages ruled for MS. Notes.

So many cherished Bibles, inconveniently crowded with brief records of study and instruction, have passed through the hands of the Publishers, that, while they have admired the skill and perseverance of writers in condensing so much within such confined limits, they have longed to provide a Bible which should conveniently afford a wider scope for these Annotations.

Octavo, Cloth	1	0	0
Turkey morocco plain	1	13	6
„ or russia, tooled to order	1	17	6

An Edition of the Comprehensive Bible printed on Super-Royal Writing-Paper, with four inches of blank margin.

Imperial quarto, Cloth	1	2	0

For Specimen Pages, see the Illustrated Supplement. By post, free.

AIDS TO THE STUDY

OF THE

OLD TESTAMENT SCRIPTURES.

The Hebrew Student's Manual.

£ s. d.

CONTENTS:—Preface, 6 pp. Recommendations to the Learner, 3 pp. I. A Hebrew Grammar, 125 pp. II. A series of Hebrew Reading Lessons, analysed, 70 pp. III. The Book of Psalms, with interlineary translation; the construction of every Hebrew word being clearly indicated, and the root of each distinguished by the use of hollow and other types, 240 pp. IV. A Hebrew and English Lexicon, containing all the Hebrew and Chaldee words in the Old Testament Scriptures, 287 pp.

Foolscap octavo, Cloth 0 10 0

A Revision of the Hebrew Text of the Old Testament.

CONTENTS: — Introduction, 12 pp. Synopsis of Readings revised from critical sources; being an attempt to present a purer and more correct Text than the 'Received' one of Van der Hooght, by the aid of the best existing materials; with the principal Various Readings found in MSS., ancient Versions, Jewish Books and Writers, Parallels, Quotations, etc., 222 pp.

By Samuel Davidson, D.D.

Octavo, Cloth 0 10 6

The Analytical Hebrew Lexicon.

CONTENTS:—The Words of the entire Hebrew Scriptures are arranged just as they are found in the Sacred Text, Alphabetically, and are Grammatically explained. The student of the original has only to turn from his Bible to this Lexicon for the solution of every etymological difficulty that may obstruct his progress, and he will find, without trouble or loss of time, a complete analysis of every word, with an account of its peculiarities, and a reference to the conjugation or declension to which it may belong, or if it be irregular, to its exceptional class. Every word is also referred to its root (where its various *significations* will be found), and with the root is given a conspectus of all the words which owe their derivation to its source. This feature of the work is of considerable value, because it affords the opportunity of studying the language from another point of view; for, by turning from root to root (the roots are distinguished in the

---

For Specimen Pages, see the Illustrated Supplement. By post, free.

alphabetical order by larger types), the student may see
at a glance in what way the various nouns, adjectives,
and other parts of speech are developed from the radical
forms. Another feature of interest is the Grammatical
Introduction, which is chiefly devoted to the study of the
irregularities of the language. Here will be found, it is
believed, every single exceptional word, with a concise
explanation of its peculiarities. The words which, in
particular forms, occur but once in the Scriptures,
possess a peculiar interest, and they are very numerous.
They have all been distinguished by a small letter, which
refers to the passage of occurrence at the foot of the
page. Among other minor advantages afforded by this
Lexicon, may be mentioned, the indication, in all cases,
of the *Kamets-Chatuph*, which requires some familiarity
with the language to distinguish.

The ANALYTICAL LEXICON is thus:—I. A Lexicon
in the ordinary sense of supplying the various meanings
of the various roots;—II. A Dictionary of every deriva-
tive and modification of every root, in alphabetical order,
with analysis;—III. A storehouse of the anomalies of
the language, carefully arranged and referred to from all
parts of the work;—IV. A Concordance of the least
easily understood words.

"It is the *ultimatum* of Hebrew Lexicography, and will
leave the Theologian, who still remains ignorant of the Sacred
tongue, absolutely without excuse."—*Churchman's Monthly
Review.*

By Professor B. Davidson.

Quarto, Cloth 1 5 0

Gesenius's Hebrew Grammar.

Enlarged and improved by Professor E. Rödiger. With
a Hebrew Reading Book, 275 pp.

Quarto, Cloth 0 7 6

With Lloyd's Analysis of Gen. I.-XL (See page 3L)   0 10 6

Gesenius's Hebrew Lexicon.

CONTENTS:—Preface, 4 pp. Address to the Student, 4 pp. Table of Alphabets, 2 pp. The Lexicon,
884 pp. English-Hebrew Index, 35 pp.

By S. P. Tregelles, LL.D.

Quarto, Cloth 1 1 0

Gesenius's Hebrew Lexicon.   Abridged Edition.

Small Quarto. *(In the Press.)*

Hebrew Reading Lessons.

CONTENTS:—Introductory Notice, 6 pp. The first
four chapters of the Book of Genesis, and the eighth

chapter of the Proverbs, with a Grammatical Praxis, and an Interlineary Translation, 70 *pp.*
By S. P. Tregelles, LL.D.
    Foolscap octavo, Cloth ..   ..   ..   0 3 6   £ *s. d.*

The Heads of Hebrew Grammar.

CONTENTS:—Preface, 8 *pp.* The Heads of Hebrew Grammar, containing all the Principles needed by a Learner, 128 *pp.;* with a Series of Hebrew Paradigms.
By S. P. Tregelles, LL.D.
    Foolscap octavo, Cloth 0 3 0

A Methodization of the Hebrew Verbs.

CONTENTS:—This original plan includes the verbs, regular and irregular, 32 *pp.*
By the Rev. Tresham D. Gregg, D.D.
    Octavo, Boards 0 1 6

A Practical Hebrew Grammar.

CONTENTS:— Preface and Introduction, 10 *pp.* The Grammar with progressive constructive Exercises to every Rule; and a Reading Book, 201 *pp.*
By Dr. J. Robert Wolfe.
    Post octavo, Cloth 0 6 0

A Pocket Hebrew-English Lexicon.

CONTENTS:—Preface, 5 *pp.* The Lexicon containing all the Hebrew and Chaldee words in the Old Testament Scriptures, with their meanings in English, and combining the alphabetical with the radical arrangement of the words, 287 *pp.*
    Foolscap octavo, Cloth 0 4 6

A Hebrew and English Bible. In Parallel Columns.

    Quarto, Cloth 0 11 0

The Hebrew Bible of the Polyglot Series.

CONTENTS:—The Hebrew Text after Van der Hooght, with the *Keri* and *Chetib,* 585 *pp.* The Various Readings of the Samaritan Pentateuch, 50 *pp.*
    Foolscap octavo, Cloth 0 10 0

Hebrew and English Old Testament, interpaged.

    Foolscap octavo, Cloth 0 18 0
    With GREEK and ENGLISH NEW TESTAMENT, extra   0 6 0

For Specimen Pages, see the Illustrated Supplement. By post, free.

		£	s.	d.
Hebrew Bible, interpaged with the Greek Septuagint.				
Foolscap octavo, Cloth		1	0	0
Hebrew and Latin Vulgate Old Testament, interpaged.				
Foolscap octavo, Cloth		0	14	6
Hebrew and German Old Testament, interpaged.				
Foolscap octavo, Cloth		0	14	6
Hebrew and French Old Testament, interpaged.				
Foolscap octavo, Cloth		0	14	6
Hebrew and Italian Old Testament, interpaged.				
Foolscap octavo, Cloth		0	14	6
Hebrew and Spanish Old Testament, interpaged.				
Foolscap octavo, Cloth		0	14	6
Hebrew and Portuguese Old Testament, interpaged.				
Foolscap octavo, Cloth		0	14	6

The Hebrew Pentateuch.

CONTENTS:— The five Books of Moses in Hebrew, with points, 140 *pp.*

Foolscap octavo, Cloth .. .. — 0 2 6

The Prophecy of Joel.

The Hebrew Text of Joel printed metrically, with a new English Translation and Critical Notes. By the Rev. Joseph Hughes, M.A.

Foolscap octavo .. .. — 0 2 6

The Apocrypha, Greek and English. In Parallel Columns.

Quarto, Cloth .. .. — 0 6 0

The Hexaplar Psalter.

CONTENTS:—The Book of Psalms in Hebrew; the Greek of the LXX.; the Vulgate Latin; Jerome's Hebrew-Latin; the English Liturgical Version; and the English Authorised Version: in six Parallel Columns, 287 *pp.*

Quarto, Cloth .. .. — 0 15 0

For Specimen Pages see the Illustrated Supplement. By post, free.

An Interlineary Hebrew-English Psalter.   £ s. d.

CONTENTS:—The Book of Psalms in Hebrew, printed
so as to distinguish the servile letters from the radical;
with a closely literal English Translation under each
word. 240 pp.

    Foolscap octavo, Cloth 0 5 0

Hebrew Psalms, without points.

    Foolscap octavo 0 1 0

Hebrew and English Psalms, with points.

    Foolscap octavo 0 1 0

Hebrew and English Psalms.

The Hebrew Text is that of Van der Hooght, carefully reprinted from the edition, A.D. 1705. The English
Version is the Authorised Translation according to the
edition of A.D. 1611. Arranged in Parallel Columns, 100 pp.

    Foolscap octavo, Cloth 0 4 0

The Epistle to the Hebrews in Hebrew.

Intended as a Tract for distribution among the Jews.

    Foolscap octavo, sewed 0 0 1
                Per 100   ..   ..   ..   1 5 0
                Per 1000   ..   ..   ..   10 0 0

**Rabbi Mosis Maimonidis liber More Nebuchim, sive
Doctor Perplexorum.**
By L. Schlosberg.

    Octavo 0 7 6

An Analysis of the first eleven Chapters of Genesis;
with copious References to Gesenius's Hebrew Grammar.
By the Rev. John Lloyd, M.A.

    Quarto, Boards 0 1 6

A new Hebrew Concordance.   *In the Press.*

The Study of the Hebrew Vowel Points.
Parts I.—II.
A Series of Exercises in very large Hebrew type,
printed upon writing-paper, with space between the lines
for the addition in manuscript of the Vowel Points and
Accents.

    Quarto. Nos. 1 and 2 ..   ..   ..   each   0 0 4

For Specimen Pages, see the Illustrated Supplement. By post, free.

	£ s. d.

The Septuagint.

> CONTENTS:—An Historical Account of the Septuagint Version, and of the principal Texts in which it is current. 16 pp. The Septuagint Version of the Old Testament, according to the Vatican edition; together with the real Septuagint Version of Daniel and the Apocrypha, including the fourth Book of Maccabees. 912 pp.
>
> Octavo, Cloth 0 18 0

The Septuagint of the Pocket Polyglot Series.

> CONTENTS:—Tables of the Various Readings of the Alexandrine Text, 101 pp. The Septuagint according to the Vatican Text, 585 pp.
>
> Foolscap octavo, Cloth 0 10 0

The Septuagint and Greek New Testament.

> Foolscap octavo, Cloth 0 13 6

An English Translation of the Septuagint.

> CONTENTS:—Preface, 8 pp. Chronological Table, 3 pp. The Translation of the Septuagint Version of the Old Testament, according to the Vatican Text, into English, with Critical Notes, and the principal Various Readings of the Alexandrine Copy, 93) pp.
>
> By Sir Lancelot Charles Lee Brenton, Bart.
>
> Octavo. Two volumes, Cloth 1 1 0

The Septuagint, with an English Translation.

> In Parallel Columns. With Critical Notes and Various Readings.
>
> Quarto, Cloth 0 12 0

The Septuagint, interpaged with the Hebrew Text.

> Foolscap octavo, Cloth 1 0 0

Greek and English Bible, interpaged.

> Foolscap octavo, Cloth 0 18 0
> With GREEK and ENGLISH NEW TESTAMENT, extra   ..   0 6 0

Greek and Latin Bible, interpaged.

> Foolscap octavo, Cloth 1 0 6

Greek and German Bible, interpaged.

> Foolscap octavo, Cloth 1 0 6

For Specimen Pages, see the Illustrated Supplement. By post, free.

	£	s.	d.

Greek and French Bible, interpaged.
    Foolscap octavo, Cloth   1   0   6

Greek and Italian Bible, interpaged.
    Foolscap octavo, Cloth   1   0   6

Greek and Spanish Bible, interpaged.
    Foolscap octavo, Cloth   1   0   6

Greek and Portuguese Bible, interpaged.
    Foolscap octavo, Cloth   1   0   6

Arabic Reading Lessons.
    CONTENTS:— Extracts from the Koran and other sources, grammatically analysed and translated; with the Elements of Arabic Grammar, 134 *pp.*
    Post octavo, Cloth   0   3   6

Chaldee Reading Lessons.
    CONTENTS:—Preface, 2 *pp.* The whole of the Biblical Chaldee, with a Grammatical Praxis and an Interlineary Translation, 140 *pp.* A series of Chaldee Paradigms.
    Foolscap octavo, Cloth   0   3   6

The Proper Names of the Old Testament, expounded and illustrated.
    CONTENTS:—A Dictionary of all the Proper Names occurring in the Old Testament Scriptures, in which these names are etymologically and hermeneutically investigated, 382 *pp.*
    By the Rev. Alfred Jones.
    Quarto, Cloth   0   15   0

The Hebrew Language.
    CONTENTS:—Preface, 6 *pp.* The History and Characteristics of the Hebrew Language, including improved renderings of select passages in our Authorised Translation of the Old Testament, 187 *pp.*
    By Henry Craik.
    Crown octavo, Cloth   0   3   6

For Specimen Pages, see the Illustrated Supplement. By post, free.

4

Principia Hebraica.   £ *s. d.*

> CONTENTS:—Preface, 2 pp. The Principles of Hebrew Grammar, 7 pp. An easy Introduction to the Hebrew Language, in twenty-four large folio Tables, which contain the Interpretation of all the Hebrew and Chaldee words, both Primitives and Derivatives, contained in the Old Testament Scriptures.
> By Henry Craik.
> Folio, Cloth   0 10 6

The Englishman's Hebrew and Chaldee Concordance of the Old Testament:

> Being an attempt at a Verbal Connection between the Original and the English Translation; with Indexes, a List of the Proper Names, and their occurrences, etc.
> Third Edition. Two volumes.
> Royal octavo, Cloth   3 13 6

The Hebraist's Vade Mecum:

> A first attempt at a Complete Verbal Index to the Contents of the Hebrew and Chaldee Scriptures. Arranged according to Grammar: the occurrences in full.
> Demy octavo   0 15 0

How to Learn to Read the Hebrew Bible, Without Points, in Twelve Lessons.

> Compiled from various sources.
> By William Penn, F.R.A.S.
> Foolscap octavo   0 1 0

The Book of Jonah :

> The Text Analyzed, Translated, and the Accents named; being an easy introduction to the Hebrew language.
> By the Rev. Alexander Mitchell, M.A.
> Octavo   0 5 0

For Specimen Pages, see the Illustrated Supplement. By post, free.

AIDS TO THE STUDY
OF THE
NEW TESTAMENT SCRIPTURES.

£ s. d.

The English Hexapla.

CONTENTS:—The Six principal English Versions of the New Testament, in Parallel Columns, beneath the Greek Original Text. The advantages of this arrangement are obvious. The meaning of the Original is reflected from the renderings of six independent Translations on the same page.
One very handsome volume.

Quarto, Cloth .. .. | 2 2 0
Turkey morocco plain .. .. .. | 3 4 0
. A few large-paper copies, Cloth .. .. .. | 3 3 0

The Greek Student's Manual.

CONTENTS:—I. A Practical Guide to the Greek Testament, designed for those who have no knowledge of the Greek language, 92 pp. II. The New Testament, Greek and English. 370 pp. III. A Greek and English Lexicon to the New Testament. 208 pp.
Foolscap octavo, Cloth .. .. | 0 10 0

A Practical Guide to the Greek New Testament.

Designed for those who have no knowledge of the Greek language, but who desire to read the New Testament in the original. 92 pp.
Foolscap octavo, Cloth .. .. | 0 2 0

A Grammar of the New Testament Dialect.

CONTENTS:—Introduction, 8 pp. A Treatise on the Grammar of the New Testament; embracing observations on the literal interpretation of numerous passages, 218 pp. Index of passages particularly noticed, 6 pp.
By the Rev. T. S. Green, M.A.
Crown octavo, Cloth .. .. | 0 7 0

Critical Notes on the New Testament.

CONTENTS:—These Notes are mainly grammatical, but their plan embraces observations on the meaning of particular terms, especially synonyms. The arrangement of sentences is treated as a matter of material importance to exact interpretation. 200 pp.
By the Rev. T. S. Green, M.A.
Crown octavo, Cloth .. .. | 0 7 0

The Analytical Greek Lexicon to the New Testament.

CONTENTS:—Tables of the Declensions and Conjugations, with explanatory grammatical remarks. 46 pp. A Dictionary, consisting of an Alphabetical arrangement of every occurring inflexion of every word contained in the

	£	s.	d.

Greek New Testament Scriptures, with a grammatical analysis of each word, and copious Lexicography, 444 pp. The Student of the Greek New Testament has only to turn to this Lexicon for the solution of every etymological difficulty that may obstruct his progress; and he will find, without trouble or loss of time, a complete analysis of every word, with an account of its peculiarities, and a reference to the conjugation or declension to which it may belong, or if it be irregular to its exceptional class.

Quarto, Cloth 0 11 0

Developed Criticism of the New Testament.

CONTENTS:—Introduction, 10 pp. A series of complete critical discussions on those passages of the New Testament which are materially affected by Various Readings, 192 pp.

By the Rev. T. S. Green, M.A.
Octavo, Cloth 0 7 0

A Pocket Greek-English Lexicon to the New Testament.

By the Rev. T. S. Green, M.A.
Foolscap octavo, Cloth 0 3 6

A Greek Concordance to the New Testament.

CONTENTS:—Address to the Reader, 3 pp. Preface. A Concordance of the words of the Greek New Testament, with their context, 280 pp.

By Erasmus Schmidt.
Foolscap octavo, Cloth 0 3 6
32mo., Cloth 0 3 6

Greenfield's Greek Lexicon to the New Testament.

CONTENTS:—Engraved Tables of Greek Numerals, and of the Ligatures or Abbreviations in Ancient Greek MSS. and Editions. The Lexicon, in which the various senses of the words are distinctly explained in English, and authorised by references to passages of Scripture, 88 pp.

Foolscap octavo, Cloth 0 2 6

Ditto.
32mo., Cloth 0 2 6

The New Testament, Greek and English.

In Parallel Columns. With Various Readings.
Quarto, Cloth 0 7 0

The Greek New Testament.

Edited from Ancient Authorities (with the Latin Version of Jerome, from the Codex Amiatinus).
By S. P. Tregelles, LL.D.
Quarto, Cloth 3 13 6

For Specimen Pages, see the Illustrated Supplement. By post, free.

	£ s. d.

A Greek Harmony of the Four Gospels.

> CONTENTS:—Preface, 4 pp. Introduction, 216 pp. The Harmony, comprising a Synopsis and a Diatessaron, with Various Readings, Parallel References, Critical Notes, Indexes, Explanatory Tables, etc., 384 pp.
> By William Stroud, M.D.
> Quarto, Cloth 0 15 0

A Large Print Greek New Testament.

> CONTENTS:—In selecting a Text to be used in this edition, *Mill's* has been preferred, as being that which is most current in this country.
> The margin contains certain of the readings which have been adopted by Griesbach, Scholz, Lachmann, or Tischendorf: the abbreviations of the names of these critics (Gb. Sch. Ln. Tf.) are subjoined to the readings which they adopt.
> A selection of references to parallel passages has also been placed in the margin: these have not been chosen without careful examination, so that they will be found, it is believed, really illustrative of the Sacred Text.
> In the four Gospels the numbers of the Ammonian Sections and the references to the Eusebian Canons have been placed in the margin; for the convenience, however, of the reader, the Greek numerals have been changed into those in common use,—the Ammonian Sections being indicated by Arabic numerals, and the Eusebian Canons by Roman. 512 pp.
> Octavo, Cloth 0 12 0

An Etymological Vocabulary of all the Words in the Greek New Testament.

> CONTENTS:—Part I. Roots. The Nouns, Adjectives, Verbs. The Hebrew words, Latin words, and roots of compound words. Part II. Derivatives and Compounds. The Substantives, Adjectives, Verbs, Pronouns, Prepositions, Conjunctions, Adverbs, and Interjections, 221 pp.
> Foolscap octavo, Cloth 0 2 6

The Englishman's Greek Concordance of The New Testament :

> Being an attempt at a Verbal connection between the Greek and the English Texts; including a Concordance to the Proper Names; with Indexes, Greek-English and English-Greek.
> Sixth Edition.
> Royal octavo, Cloth 1 1 0

For Specimen Pages, see the Illustrated Supplement. By post, free.

	£	s.	d.

The Twofold New Testament.

CONTENTS:—A newly-formed Greek Text, with an accompanying new Translation into English. In Parallel Columns, 460 pp.

By the Rev. T. S. Green, M.A.

"I have taken some pains to produce, as far as possible, a strict uniformity of the rendering of terms; so that the mere English reader may have presented to him the sameness and difference of expression which are found in the Original, as far as this can be fairly done." (Preface.)

Quarto, Cloth   ..   .. | 1 | 1 | 0 |

A Collation of the Critical Texts of Griesbach, Scholz, Lachmann, and Tischendorf, with the Received Text, 90 pp.

By S. P. Tregelles, LL.D.

. Octavo, Sewed   ..   .. | 0 | 1 | 0 |

Pocket Critical Greek and English New Testament.

CONTENTS:—The Greek Text of Scholz, with the Readings, both textual and marginal, of Griesbach, and the variations of the editions of Stephens, 1550; Beza, 1598; and the Elzevir, 1633; with the English Authorised Version, and its marginal renderings, 624 pp.

16mo., Cloth   ..   .. | 0 | 6 | 0 |

With GREEK-ENGLISH LEXICON, extra.

A Greek and English New Testament for MS. Notes.

This is an edition of the last, printed upon writing-paper, with broad margins for Annotations.

Quarto, Cloth   ..   .. | 0 | 7 | 6 |

The Traveller's New Testament.

The object of this volume is to provide the Christian Student with the greatest possible help in the most portable form.

CONTENTS:—The New Testament Scriptures, in Greek and English, with Various Readings, and a complete Lexicon.

Pocket volume, Bound in the best morocco, limp and flexible, with projecting edges and a protecting flap, secured with an elastic band ..   .. | 0 | 15 | 0 |

For Specimen Pages, see the Illustrated Supplement. By post, free.

The Analytical Greek Testament:

 Presenting at one view the Text of Scholz and a Grammatical Analysis of the Verbs, in which every occurring inflection of Verb or Participle is minutely described and traced to its proper Root. With the Readings Textual and Marginal of Griesbach; and the variations of Stephens, 1550; Beza, 1598; the Elzevir, 1633.

 Square 16mo. *(Nearly ready.)* .. .. .. | 0 12 0

The Polymicrian Greek New Testament.

 CONTENTS:—The Received Greek Text, with Various Readings, Parallel References, indication of the Roots, Maps, engraved Tables, etc., 605 pp.

 32mo., Cloth .. .. | 0 3 6

A Thin Pocket Greek New Testament.

 CONTENTS:—Preface, 2 pp. Griesbach's Various Readings, 22 pp. The Greek New Testament according to Mill's edition of the Received Text, 188 pp.

 Foolscap octavo, Cloth .. .. | 0 3 6

 With this edition of the New Testament may be bound up a Greek Lexicon and a Greek Concordance.

The Narrow Greek New Testament.

 CONTENTS:—The Text of Scholz, with the Readings, both textual and marginal, of Griesbach; and the variations of the editions of Stephens, 1550; Beza, 1598; the Elzevir, 1633, 656 pp.

 32mo. .. .. | 0 4 6

Greek and English New Testament, interpaged.

 Foolscap octavo, Cloth .. .. | 0 6 0

Greek and Latin New Testament, interpaged.

 Foolscap octavo, Cloth .. .. | 0 6 0

Greek and German New Testament, interpaged.

 Foolscap octavo, Cloth .. .. | 0 6 0

Greek and Italian New Testament, interpaged.

 Foolscap octavo, Cloth .. .. | 0 6 0

Greek and Spanish New Testament, interpaged.

 Foolscap octavo, Cloth .. .. | 0 6 0

Greek and French New Testament, interpaged.

 Foolscap octavo, Cloth .. .. | 0 6 0

Greek and Portuguese New Testament, interpaged.

 Foolscap octavo, Cloth .. .. | 0 6 0

	£ s. d.
Greek and Hebrew New Testament, interpaged.	
Foolscap octavo, Cloth	0 7 0
A Hebrew Version of the New Testament.	
By William Greenfield.	
Octavo, Cloth	0 6 0
Ditto.	
Foolscap octavo, Cloth	0 3 6
Ditto. *Polymicrian Edition.*	
32mo, Cloth	0 3 6
The Acts, Greek and English, for MS. Notes.	
Small quarto, Cloth	0 1 6
St. John's Gospel, Epistles, and Prophecy.	
CONTENTS:—The complete Writings of the Apostle John, printed in Greek and English on opposite pages, 187 pp.	
Foolscap octavo, Cloth '..	0 5 0
The Codex Montfortianus.	
CONTENTS:—Preface, 20 pp. Introduction, 64 pp. A Collation of this celebrated MS. throughout the Gospels and Acts, with the Greek Text of Wetstein, and with certain MSS. in the University of Oxford, 190 pp.	
By Orlando T. Dobbin, LL.D.	
Octavo, Antique cloth	0 10 6
The Codex Zacynthius.	
"Even on a cursory examination, the value of the MS. appeared to be great; but as in many parts it was illegible, except in a very good light, and as it would take a considerable time to decipher the Biblical portion, I made application to the Committee, through the Rev. John Mee, one of the Secretaries, for permission to use the MS. at my own abode. This was kindly granted me, and thus I have been able to collate the MS., and to prepare the portion containing the text of St. Luke for publication, with a facsimile of the entire page, text and Catena.	
"I do not know of any MS. of equal antiquity accompanied by a Catena; in many respects this most valuable palimpsest is worthy of special attention; it is remarkable that it had remained in this country for nearly forty years unread and unused."	
By S. P. Tregelles, LL.D.	
Folio, Half-russia	1 1 0

For Specimen Pages, see the Illustrated Supplement. By post, free.

	£ s. d.
An Account of the Printed Text of the Greek N.T. With Remarks on its Revision upon Critical principles.	

CONTENTS:—Preface, 4 pp. Index of passages the reading of which is discussed or noticed, 2 pp. An account of the Complutensian edition:—the editions of Erasmus:—the editions of Stephens, Beza, and the Elzevirs:—Walton's Polyglot, and Bishop Fell's Greek Testament:—Mill's Greek Testament:—Bentley's proposed edition:—Bengel, Wetstein, Griesbach, Scholz, Lachmann's editions—Tischendorf's editions:—an Estimate of MS. Authorities:—Collations and Critical Studies of S. P. Tregelles:—Principles of Textual Criticism:—Passages of Dogmatic importance:—Conclusion, 274 pp. A Collation of the Critical Texts of Griesbach, Scholz, Lachmann, and Tischendorf, with that in common use, 94 pp.

By S. P. Tregelles, LL.D.

Octavo, Cloth .. .. | 0 10 6

Syriac Reading Lessons.

CONTENTS:—Extracts from the Peschito Version of the Old and New Testaments; and the Crusade of Richard I., from the Chronicles of Bar Hebræus; grammatically analysed and translated: with the Elements of Syriac Grammar, 123 pp.

Post octavo, Cloth .. .. | 0 3 6

Syriac and English New Testament.

Small Quarto. *(In the Press.)*

The Syriac New Testament.

Post octavo, Cloth .. .. | 0 8 0

Turkey morocco plain .. .. .. | 0 16 0

A Syriac Lexicon to the New Testament.

By E. Henderson. Ph.D.

Post octavo, Cloth .. .. | 0 2 6

A Samaritan Grammar.

CONTENTS:—Introduction. 13 pp. The Grammar of the Samaritan Language, with Extracts and Vocabulary, 132 pp.

By G. F. Nicholls.

Post octavo, Cloth .. .. | 0 6 0

For Specimen Pages, see the Illustrated Supplement. By post, free.

The Genevan New Testament.

£ s. d.

CONTENTS:—The Epistle declaring that Christ is the end of the Law, by John Calvin, 16 pp. To the Reader, Mercie and Peace through Christ our Saviour, 5 pp. The New Testament, being an exact and accurate representation of the Edition of 1557, with the marginal annotations and references, the initial and other woodcuts, Prefaces and Index, 910 pp.

Quarto, large paper copies, Cloth .. .. .. | 1 10 0

The Seven Epistles and Revelation.

CONTENTS:— Introduction, 18 pp. An Original Translation of the Epistles of James, Peter, John, and Jude; and the Book of Revelation; with Critical Notes, 60 pp.
By Joseph Turnbull, Ph.D.
Octavo, Cloth .. .. | 0 4 6

The Epistles of Paul the Apostle.

CONTENTS:—Introduction, 35 pp. An Original Translation, with Critical Notes, 146 pp.
By Joseph Turnbull, Ph.D.
Octavo, Cloth .. .. | 0 7 0

The Revelation, from Ancient Authorities.

CONTENTS:—Preface, 6 pp. Address to the Reader, 23 pp. The Book of Revelation, translated from the Greek Text, according to the Ancient Authorities; so that there is not a single word which is not guaranteed by MS. authority of at least 1200 years old. 44 pp. Prospectus of a Critical Edition of the Greek New Testament, with an Historical Sketch of the Printed Text, 33 pp. Description of a Palimpsest MS. hitherto unused, 4 pp.
By S. P. Tregelles, LL.D.
Foolscap octavo, Limp cloth .. .. | 0 2 0

An amended Translation of the Hebrews.

CONTENTS:— Preface, 4 pp. The Epistle to the Hebrews, 29 pp. Notes explanatory of the altered renderings, 10 pp.
By Henry Craik.
Foolscap octavo, Sewed .. .. .. | 0 0 6

The Gospel of Matthew in Arabic.

Printed with all the vowels, on a new and simpler plan, with an Introduction explanatory of the method of printing the Arabic vowels, both mechanically and philologically.
By the Rev. Jules Ferrette, Missionary at Damascus.
Foolscap octavo, Cloth .. .. | 0 3 0

	£ s. d.

The Narrow Gospels.

CONTENTS:—The four Gospels, according to the Authorised Version, printed in a narrow shape to secure the utmost portability.

32mo. Roan 0 2 6
     Turkey morocco limp 0 5 0

The Narrow Epistles.

CONTENTS:—The Epistles, according to the Authorised Version, printed in a narrow shape to secure the utmost portability.

32mo., Limp roan 0 2 6
     Turkey morocco limp 0 5 0

Historic Evidence of the New Testament.

CONTENTS:—Introduction, 16 pp. A Lecture on the Historic Evidence of the Authorship and Transmission of the Books of the New Testament, 96 pp. Appendix, No. I. On the Text of the New Testament. No. II. Some of the results of the genuineness of the New Testament. 34 pp.

By S. P. Tregelles, LL.D.

Post octavo, Cloth 0 3 0

Improved Renderings of the New Testament.

CONTENTS:— Preface, 4 pp. Introduction, 8 pp. Hints to Students, 2 pp. Improved Renderings of those passages of the New Testament which are capable of being more correctly translated, 40 pp.

By Henry Craik.

Crown octavo, Cloth 0 1 0

Textual Criticism of the New Testament.

CONTENTS:— Introduction, 4 pp. A succinct comparison of the Authorised Version of the New Testament with the critical Texts of Griesbach, Scholz, Lachmann, Tischendorf, Tregelles, and Alford, including the Codex Sinaiticus, 34 pp.

By C. E. Stuart, Esq.

16mo. and Octavo, Cloth .. .. each 0 3 0

For Specimen Pages, see the Illustrated Supplement. By post, free.

£ s. d.

A Revised New Testament.

CONTENTS:—Preface, 8 pp. A Revised Translation of the New Testament, with a notice of the principal Various Headings in the Greek Text, 532 pp.
By the Rev. H. Highton, M.A.

Octavo, Cloth 0 10 6

A Critical English New Testament,

presenting at one view the Authorised Version and the Results of the latest criticism of the Original Text.

The Authorised Version is printed unaltered, but in those passages in which it will be necessary in adapting the Translation to a restored Greek Text to *omit* certain words, such words are inclosed between brackets. In all cases where it will be necessary to *add* anything to the Authorised Version, such additions are given between brackets, and in italic type. And wherever the restoration of the Original necessitates an alteration of the expression, the fact is brought under the reader's notice by very simple and obvious typographical arrangements.

It has been thought desirable in a matter of such solemn importance as the attempted rectification of the New Testament Scriptures, to adduce in every instance the critical authority upon which every proposed alteration rests. When the remarkable agreement in judgment of the Editors whose recensions have been adopted as the basis of this Critical English New Testament (although they have arrived at their results by slightly different principles), is observed, there is abundant ground for confidence that the Greek Text to which we now happily have access, really represents in a high degree of exactitude the veritable Word of God. Second Edition.

Octavo, Cloth 0 3 6

The New Testament,

According to the Authorised Version; with Analysis, Notes, etc.

Designed to put the English reader in possession of the accuracies and perfections of the Inspired Original.

In paragraphs; with the subject of each paragraph given in the margin: and with suggestions for improved renderings, with proofs. Altered tenses of verbs restored.

For Specimen Pages, see the Illustrated Supplement. By post, free.

		£ s. d.
Indications of the presence or absence of the Greek article. Emphatic pronouns marked. Revised references; and other features. By Thomas Newberry.		
Cloth boards		0 11 6
Extra Cloth		0 13 6

The Emphasised New Testament:

Newly translated, from the Text of Tregelles, and critically emphasised according to the logical idiom of the original by means of underscored lines. With an Introduction and occasional Notes.

"THE EMPHASISED NEW TESTAMENT" is marked by the following features:—

1. It distinguishes all emphatic words.

2. It shows every recurrence of the Greek Article, whether translated or not.

3. It pays special heed to the Moods and Tenses.

4. It endeavours to render theological and ecclesiastical terms according to their simple meaning.

5. It is an entirely Independent Translation, formed directly from the Greek, and is in no sense a mere Revision.

6. It has been faithfully executed from the Text of Tregelles.

7. It contains an Introduction treating of Emphasis, the Greek Article, and the Tenses.

8. It has occasional brief suggestive Notes.

"Designed for the private use of studious readers, this Translation, of set purpose, adheres more closely to the idiom of the original than a Version intended for public use could have done with propriety. Especially in respect of EMPHASIS has an endeavour been made to enable the English reader to perceive the point and energy which are everywhere, in the Greek, revealed simply by the arrangement of words and clauses. Not only is the emphatic *effect* of that arrangement uniformly marked in this Translation by careful UNDERSCORING, but as much of the emphatic *idiom itself* is reproduced as seemed likely to meet with thoughtful appreciation." The Introduction discusses, not only the Laws of "Emphasis," but also "The Power of the Greek Article," and "The Forces of the various Tenses," —to all of which careful regard has been paid by the Translator. The Notes, though occasional and brief, are suggestive, and it is hoped will incite the reader to discover for himself many valuable hints conveyed by the Emphasised Text.

By Joseph B. Rotherham.

		£ s. d.
Octavo, Cloth		0 7 6

For Specimen Pages, see the Illustrated Supplement. By post, free.

	£	s.	d.
The Vulgate New Testament, Compared with the Douay Version of 1582. In Parallel Columns. Small Quarto, Cloth	0	6	0
A Spur and Encouragement. CONTENTS :—An incentive to the Study of the Greek Testament, with some practical Suggestions for Learners, 20 *pp.* Octavo. Sewed	0	0	6
The Reason Why all Christians should read God's written Word in Greek : and demonstration afforded of the ease with which an accurate knowledge thereof may be gained by those who have not had a classical education. Octavo. Sewed	0	0	6
How to Learn to Read the Greek New Testament. Compiled from various sources. By William Penn, F.R.A.S. Foolscap octavo	0	3	6
The Gospel according to St. Matthew, Greek and English, for MS. Notes. Printed upon writing-paper, with broad margins for Annotations. Quarto, Cloth	0	1	6

For Specimen Pages, see the Illustrated Supplement. By post, free.

NEW TESTAMENTS.

	£	s.	d.
English New Testament, thin edition.			
Octavo, Turkey morocco limp	0	10	0
Ditto.			
Foolscap octavo, Turkey morocco limp	0	6	6
Ditto.			
16mo., Turkey morocco limp	0	5	6
A Narrow English New Testament.			
32mo., Roan	0	6	0
Turkey morocco limp	0	9	0
„ „ „ with flaps	0	12	0
The Polymicrian English New Testament.			
32mo., Cloth (Half-morocco to order.)	0	2	6
Turkey morocco plain	0	6	6
„ „ hand tooled	0	9	0
The Large-Print Paragraph New Testament.			
See page 24.			
Crown octavo, Cloth	0	12	0
Turkey morocco plain ..	1	0	0
The Triglot Gospels.			
Contents: The Four Gospels in Greek, Syriac, and Latin, 310 pp. Various Readings of the Greek Text, 24 pp.			
Quarto, Cloth	0	14	0
The Enneaglot New Testament.			
Contents:—The New Testament Scriptures in Greek, Latin, English, Hebrew, French, German, Italian, Portuguese, and Spanish, 1700 pp.			
Foolscap octavo, Cloth	0	15	0
A Polyglot New Testament.			
Contents:—Prolegomena, 75 pp. The New Testament in Greek, Syriac, Latin, Portuguese, and English, 667 pp.			
By Professor Samuel Lee.			
Quarto, Cloth	0	12	0

For Specimen Pages, see the Illustrated Supplement. By post, free.

SPECIMEN PAGES OF THE BOOK OF
COMMON PRAYER AND CHURCH SERVICES.

III. MORNING PRAYER.

the same, by his infinite goodness and mercy. And although we ought at all times humbly to acknowledge our sins before God; not the death of a sinner, but rather that he may turn from his wickedness, and live; and hath given power, and commandment, to his Minis-

II. MORNING PRAYER.

the same, by his infinite goodness and mercy. And although we his wickedness, and live; and hath given power, and commandment,

I. MORNING PRAYER.

and the truth is not in us; but if we confess our sins, he is faithful and just to forgive us our sins, and to cleanse us from all unrighteousness. 1 St. John i. 8, 9.

DEARLY beloved brethren, the Scripture moveth us in sundry places to acknowledge and confess our manifold sins and wickedness; and that we should not dissemble nor cloke them before the face of Almighty God our heavenly Father; but confess them with an humble, lowly, penitent, and obedient heart; to the end that we may obtain forgiveness of the same, by his infinite goodness and mercy. And although we ought at all times humbly to acknowledge our sins before God; yet ought we most chiefly so to do, when we assemble and meet together to render thanks for the great benefits that we have received at his hands, to set forth his most worthy praise, to hear his most holy Word, and to ask those things which are requisite and necessary, as well for the body as the soul. Wherefore I pray and beseech you, as many as are here present, to accompany me with a pure heart, and humble voice, unto the throne of the heavenly grace, saying after me;

¶ A general Confession,
to be said of the whole Congregation after the Minister, all kneeling.

ALMIGHTY and most merciful Father; We have erred, and strayed from thy ways like lost sheep. We have followed too much the devices and desires of our own hearts. We have offended against thy holy laws. We have left undone those things which we ought to have done; And we have done those things which we ought not to have done; And there is no health in us. But thou, O Lord, have mercy upon us, miserable offenders. Spare thou them, O God, which confess their faults. Restore thou them that are penitent; According to thy promises declared unto mankind in Christ Jesu our Lord. And grant, O most merciful Father, for his sake; That we may hereafter live a godly, righteous, and sober life, To the glory of thy holy Name. Amen.

¶ The Absolution, or Remission of Sins.

ALMIGHTY God, the Father of our Lord Jesus Christ, who desireth not the death of a sinner,

ters, to declare and pronounce to his people being penitent, the Absolution and Remission of their sins; He pardoneth and absolveth all them that truly repent, and unfeignedly believe his holy Gospel.

Wherefore let us beseech him to grant us true repentance and his holy Spirit, that those things may please him which we do at this present; and that the rest of our life hereafter may be pure, and holy; so that at the last we may come to his eternal through us Christ our Lord.

CHURCH SERVICES, Etc.

(I.) Imperial 32mo. Church Services.

With Hymns Ancient and Modern, extra.
Seconds morocco, stiff and limp.
    „   „   old style.
Turkey morocco plain.
    „   „   hand-tooled.
    „   „   limp circuit.
Green russia, limp circuit, red under gilt edges.
Levant morocco, old style.
    „   „   „   tooled, Oxford Cross.
    „   „   richly tooled, antique pattern, tooled edges.

(II.) Emerald Church Services.

With Hymns Ancient and Modern, extra.
Seconds morocco, stiff and limp.
    „   „   old style.
Turkey morocco plain.
    „   „   hand tooled.
    „   „   limp circuit.
Green russia, limp circuit, red under gilt edges.
Levant morocco, old style.
    „   „   „   tooled, Oxford Cross.
    „   „   richly tooled, antique pattern, tooled edges.

(III.) Brevier Foolscap Church Services.

With Hymns Ancient and Modern, extra.
Seconds morocco, stiff and limp.
    „   „   old style.
Turkey morocco plain.
    „   „   hand tooled.
    „   „   limp circuit.
Green russia, limp circuit, red under gilt edges.
Levant morocco, old style.
    „   „   „   tooled Oxford Cross.
    „   „   richly tooled, antique pattern, tooled edges.

Prices may be obtained, and Specimens seen, at all the principal Booksellers, and at SAMUEL BAGSTER AND SONS.

For Specimen Pages, see page 68.

Red Rubric Church Services.   *Crown octavo.*

With HYMNS ANCIENT AND MODERN, extra.
This Edition is printed on fine toned paper.
Seconds morocco, stiff and limp.
    "   "   old style.
Turkey morocco plain.
    "   "   hand tooled.
    "   "   limp circuit.
Green russia, limp circuit, red under gilt edges.
Levant morocco, old style.
    "   "   "   tooled, Oxford Cross.
    "   "   richly tooled, antique pattern,
                                  tooled edges.
Eight Beautiful Illustrations, 3s. extra.

THE BOOK OF COMMON PRAYER.

(I.) Imperial 32mo. Common Prayer.

With HYMNS ANCIENT AND MODERN, extra.
Seconds morocco, stiff and limp.
Turkey morocco plain.
    "   "   hand tooled.
    "   "   limp circuit.
Green russia, limp circuit, red under gilt edges.
Levant morocco, old style.
    "   "   "   tooled, Oxford Cross
    "   "   richly tooled, antique pattern,
                                  tooled edges.

(II.) Emerald Common Prayer.

With HYMNS ANCIENT AND MODERN, extra.
Seconds morocco, stiff and limp.
Turkey morocco plain.
    "   "   hand tooled.
    "   "   limp circuit.
Green russia, limp circuit, red under gilt edges.
Levant morocco, old style.
    "   "   "   tooled, Oxford Cross
    "   "   richly tooled, antique pattern,
                                  tooled edges.

Prices may be obtained, and Specimens seen, at all the principal Booksellers, and at SAMUEL BAGSTER AND SONS.

For Specimen Pages, see page 42.

(III.) Brevier Foolscap Common Prayer.

With Hymns Ancient and Modern, extra.
Seconds morocco, stiff and limp.
,, ,, old style.
Turkey morocco plain.
,, ,, hand tooled.
,, ,, limp circuit.
Green russia, limp circuit, red under gilt edges.
Levant morocco, old style.
,, ,, ,, tooled, Oxford Cross.
,, ,, richly tooled, antique pattern,
tooled edges.

Red Rubric Common Prayer.   *Crown octavo.*

With Hymns Ancient and Modern, extra.
This Edition is printed on fine toned paper.
Seconds morocco, stiff or limp.
,, ,, old style.
Turkey morocco plain.
,, ,, hand tooled.
,, ,, limp circuit.
Green russia, limp circuit, red under gilt edges.
Levant morocco, old style.
,, ,, ,, tooled, Oxford Cross.
,, ,, richly tooled, antique pattern
tooled edges.

Six beautiful Illuminations, 2s. 6d. extra.

----◆----

The Octaglot Book of Common Prayer,

And Administration of the Sacraments, and other Rites
and Ceremonies of the Church, according to the use
of the Church of England: together with the Psalter,
or Psalms of David; in Eight Languages; namely,
English, French, Italian, German, Spanish, Greek
Ancient and Modern, Latin; to which are added, the
Services used at Sea; the Services for the Twentieth of
June; with the form and manner of making, ordaining,
and consecrating Bishops, Priests, and Deacons; also
the Thirty-nine Articles of Religion, in Latin and
English; and the Service used at the Convocation of the
Clergy.
Foolscap octavo, Cloth 0 12 0

For Specimen Pages, see the Illustrated Supplement. By post, free.

	£	s.	d.

Biblia Ecclesiæ Polyglotta.

> CONTENTS:—Preface, 9 pp. The Sunday Lessons from the Old Testament Scriptures, in Hebrew, Greek, Latin, and English, in Parallel Columns, 448 pp. The Book of Psalms, in Hebrew, Greek, two Latin Versions, and two English Versions, in six Parallel Columns, 211 pp. 1843.
> Edited by Frederick Iliff, D.D.

    Quarto, Cloth 0 10 0

        Turkey morocco plain, gilt edges 1 10 0

Biblia Ecclesiæ Polyglotta.

> Large-paper copies.
> Royal quarto, Cloth 1 10 0

The Offices for the Sick.

> CONTENTS:—Private Baptism of Infants; Visitation of the Sick; The Communion of the Sick (properly arranged) according to the use of the Church of England, 32 pp. Large print.

    Foolscap octavo, Cloth 0 3 0

        Turkey morocco limp 0 5 6

French Common Prayer.   *Polymicrian Edition.*

> CONTENTS:—The Book of Common Prayer, translated into French, 590 pp.

    32mo., Cloth 0 1 6

        Turkey morocco plain 0 6 0

Ditto.

    Foolscap octavo, Cloth 0 2 6

        Turkey morocco limp 0 6 6

Ditto.

> Large-print Edition.
> Octavo, Cloth 0 7 0

Latin Common Prayer.   *Polymicrian Edition.*

> •   CONTENTS:—The Book of Common Prayer, in Latin. 634 pp.
> Edited by John Carey, LL.D.

    32mo., Cloth 0 1 6

        Turkey morocco plain 0 6 0

Ditto.

    Foolscap octavo, Cloth 0 2 6

        Turkey morocco limp 0 6 6

For Specimen Pages, see the Illustrated Supplement. By post, free.

	£	s.	d.
German Common Prayer. *Polymicrian Edition.*			
CONTENTS:—The Book of Common Prayer, translated into German, 572 pp. By Dr. Küper.			
32mo., Cloth	0	2	6
Turkey morocco plain	0	6	0
Ditto.			
Foolscap octavo, Cloth	0	2	6
Turkey morocco limp	0	6	6
Italian Common Prayer. *Polymicrian Edition.*			
CONTENTS:—The Book of Common Prayer, translated into Italian, 572 pp.			
32mo., Cloth	0	2	6
Turkey morocco plain	0	6	0
Ditto.			
Foolscap octavo, Cloth	0	1	5
Turkey morocco limp	0	6	6
Spanish Common Prayer. *Polymicrian Edition.*			
CONTENTS:—The Book of Common Prayer, translated into Spanish, 572 pp. By the Rev. Blanco White.			
32mo., Cloth	0	2	6
Turkey morocco plain	0	6	0
Ditto.			
Foolscap octavo, Cloth	0	2	6
Turkey morocco limp	0	6	6
Greek Common Prayer. *Polymicrian Edition.*			
CONTENTS:—The Book of Common Prayer, in Greek, 572 pp.			
32mo., Cloth	0	2	6
Turkey morocco plain	0	6	0
Ditto.			
Foolscap octavo, Cloth	0	2	6
Turkey morocco limp	0	6	6
Modern Greek Common Prayer. *Polymicrian Edition.*			
CONTENTS:—The Book of Common Prayer, translated into modern Greek, 572 pp. By A. Calbo.			
32mo., Cloth	0	2	6
Turkey morocco plain	0	6	0

For Specimen Pages, see the Illustrated Supplement. By post, free.

The Revised Liturgy of 1689.

CONTENTS:— Introduction, 6 pp. The Book of Common Prayer, interleaved with the alterations prepared for Convocation by the Royal Commissioners, in the first year of the reign of William and Mary, 192 pp. By John Taylor, Esq.
Octavo, Cloth 0 6 6

PSALTERS, ETC.

The Hexaplar Psalter, in six Parallel Columns.

CONTENTS:— The Hebrew Text, after Van der Hooght; the Greek of the LXX.; the Vulgate Latin; Jerome's Hebrew Latin; the English Liturgical Version; and the English Authorised Version, 273 pp.
Quarto, Cloth 0 15 0
Turkey morocco plain 1 10 0

Psalters, in various Languages.

English, Greek (Ancient and Modern), Latin, German, French, Italian, Spanish.
32mo., Roan, gilt edges, each 0 1 0

The Prayer Book Psalter.   Large type.

16mo., Cloth 0 1 6
Roan 0 3 0
Turkey morocco limp 0 5 6

Bible Psalms, metrically arranged.

CONTENTS:— Preface, 7 pp. Sundry Tables, 6 pp. The Book of Psalms, historically arranged, 264 pp.
12mo., Cloth 0 4 6

The Bible and Prayer Book Psalms.

CONTENTS:— Preface, 4 pp. The two versions of the Psalms, in Parallel Columns, with Notes, critical and explanatory, 200 pp.
By Sir Lancelot Charles Lee Brenton, Bart.
16mo., Cloth, red edges 0 3 0

The "Narrow" Psalms.

The Psalms according to the Authorised Version, printed in a narrow shape to secure the utmost portability.
32mo., Limp roan 0 1 6
Turkey morocco limp 0 4 6

For Specimen Pages, see the Illustrated Supplement. By post, free.

A Critical Translation of the Psalms, in Metre.   £ s. d.

> CONTENTS.—Preface, 14 pp. While regarding the
> Authorised English Version with great deference and
> respect, it has been felt that the final appeal on all occa-
> sions should be to the Hebrew text; and, at the correct
> meaning of this, the translator has spared no pains to
> arrive, by availing himself of the labours and researches
> of eminent scholars who have made Hebrew literature
> the chief study of their lives. He has also felt with
> Bishop Lowth, that it is of great importance to distin-
> guish *the system of the verses.* To discover what traces
> are left of the original versification has therefore been
> his constant endeavour; and the result of his investiga-
> tion has been, to learn, that while, in the Hebrew Psalter,
> couplets and triplets are often to be found, the quatrain,
> or stanza of four lines, greatly predominates. A few
> Psalms, however, there are, that seem to fall naturally
> into six-line stanzas, and in the Hundredth Psalm
> there is a perfect specimen of triplets. 250 pp. Notes,
> 50 pp.
>
>   Crown octavo, Cloth 0 5 6

The Bible Psalms.   Large type.

>   16mo., Cloth 0 1 6
>   Roan   ..   ..   :: 0 1 0
>   Turkey morocco limp 0 5 6

A Textual Commentary on the Psalms.

> CONTENTS.—Preface, 2 pp.   The Commentary,
> 93 pp.   In making use of this Volume, the Reader is
> supposed to have a Bible open at the Psalm which has
> been selected for meditation or study, and after having
> read a verse or single clause, to read the lines connected
> therewith in the Commentary.
> By H. N. Champney, Esq.
>   Square 16mo., Cloth 0 1 0

The Psalms, with Scripture Illustrations.

>   32mo., Roan 0 1 6
>   Turkey morocco limp 0 5 0

Bible Psalms.   *Polymicrian Edition.*

>   32mo., Roan 0 1 0

The Prayer Book Psalter, in Eight Languages.

>   Foolscap octavo, Cloth 0 4 0

For Specimen Pages, see the Illustrated Supplement.   By post, free.

ATLASES.

	£	s.	d

A Scripture Atlas.

CONTENTS:—Eighteen Maps, and Plans, with a Chronological Chart of History, from the Creation to the Fourth Century of the Christian Era.

Foolscap octavo, Cloth .. .. — 0 1 0

The Chronological School Atlas.

CONTENTS:—A complete series of Maps, elucidatory of the Sacred History; illustrating also the principal Epochs of the Ecclesiastical History of Christendom, and the condition of the Holy Land, from the earliest ages to the present day. An elaborate Chart of general History, and a comparative Index and Concordance of all the Scripture occurrences of the Places. With descriptive letterpress to each Map.

Quarto, Cloth .. .. — 0 7 6

A Scripture Atlas.

CONTENTS:—Thirty Coloured Maps, in which will be found, not only the places of well-defined situation, but the other localities of Historic interest mentioned throughout the Sacred Scriptures, according to the supposition of the best Authors. With a Geographical Index.

By J. Wyld.

Quarto, Cloth .. .. .. — 0 7 6

The Ethnographic Atlas.

CONTENTS:—I. A Map of the Countries in which the Monosyllabic Languages are spoken. II. A Geographical view of the extension of the Shemitic Languages. III. A Geographical view of the extension of the Medo-Persian Family of Languages. IV. The Sanscrit Family of Languages. V. A Map of Europe, showing the distribution of the Celtic, Teutonic, Greco-Latin, Thraco-Illyrian, and Slavonic Families. VI. The Finno-Tartarian Family of Languages. VII. The Polynesian and Negritian Languages. VIII. The native Languages of Africa. IX. A Map of the Languages of North and South America. X. A Map exhibiting the Ancient diffusion of the Hebrew language through the Phœnician Colonies.

Detailed explanations accompany each Map.

Quarto, Cloth .. .. — 0 7 6

For Specimen Pages, see the Illustrated Supplement. By post, free.

A Scripture Atlas. £ *s. d.*

CONTENTS:—I. The Lands of the Patriarchs. II. Peninsula of Sinai, with part of Egypt. III. The Lands of Edom and Moab. IV. The Mountain Wilderness of Sinai. V. Canaan before the Conquest by Joshua. VI. Canaan as divided among the Tribes. VII. The Kingdom of Judah. VIII. The Hebrew Kingdom under Solomon. IX. A Map of the Captivities. X. Babylonia and Susiana. XI. The Land of Uz, etc. XII. Phœnicia and Mount Lebanon. XIII. Nineveh. XIV. Babylon. XV. The Nile Valley. XVI. Thebes. XVII. Egypt, etc. XVIII. The Palestine of Prophecy. XIX. and XX. Comparative View of the Ancient Persian and Roman Empires. XXI. Palestine at the commencement of the Christian Era. XXII. The Sea of Galilee and its Environs. XXIII. A Plan of Jerusalem. XXIV. The Environs of Jerusalem. XXV. The Countries adjacent to the Mediterranean. XXVI. Ancient Rome. XXVII. Asia Minor during the Apostolic Period. XXVIII. The Nations of the Ancient World. XXIX. Pergamos. XXX. Thyatira. XXXI. Smyrna. XXXII. Sardis. XXXIII. Ephesus. XXXIV. Philadelphia. XXXV. Laodicea. XXXVI. Patmos.

By W. Hughes, F.R.G.S., etc.

Octavo, Cloth .. .. o 7 6

For Specimen Pages, see the Illustrated Supplement. By post, free.

MISCELLANEOUS.

	£	s.	d.
Daily Light on the Daily Path. *Large Edition.*			
Contents:—A devotional Text-book for every day in the Year, Morning and Evening; in the very words of Scripture.			
Large-print edition, 10mo. Two Volumes.			
Extra cloth, gilt edges. Each vol.	0	4	6
Bound in calf. Each vol.	0	6	0
Bound in morocco. Each vol.	0	7	0
ditto, turkey, tooled	0	8	6
ditto, with flaps	0	10	6
Daily Light on the Daily Path. *Small Edition.*			
32mo. Two Volumes.			
Extra cloth, gilt edges. Each vol.	0	1	6
Bound in calf. Each vol.	0	4	6
Bound in morocco. Each vol.	0	5	0
ditto, turkey	0	6	6
ditto, with flaps	0	7	0
Illustrated Pocket Bible,			
For the Young. Containing forty-eight Historical Pictures, with 4,000 suggestive Questions, coloured Maps, and a complete Index of Subjects.			
In attractive morocco binding	0	14	0
Four Thousand Questions, intended to open up the Scriptures to the Young.			
10mo.	0	0	6
Concise Answers			
To the Four Thousand Scripture Questions of the Illustrated Pocket Bible. For the use of Parents and Teachers.			
Foolscap octavo. Paper wrapper	0	1	0
Cloth	0	1	6
A French Reading Book,			
For Schools and Families. Being the Historical Books of the New Testament, in pure modern French.			
By Jonas Vuitel.			
Octavo, Cloth	0	3	0

For Specimen Pages, see the Illustrated Supplement. By post, free.

Prayers and Devotional Meditations,
From the Psalms of David.
By Elihu Burritt.
Octavo .. .. | 0 2 0

The Children of the Bible.
By Elihu Burritt.
32mo. .. .. | 0 0 6

An Order for Morning and Evening Prayer,

Being an abridgement of the forms in the Common
Prayer Book.
To be used by Lay Readers in Mission Rooms,
Hospitals, etc.
Sewed .. .. | 0 0 2

The Poetry of the Hebrew Pentateuch.
Being Four Essays on Moses and the Mosaic Age.
By the Rev. M. Margoliouth, M.A., LL.D., Ph.D., etc.
Octavo .. .. | 0 3 6

The Oracles of God, and their Vindication.
Being a Sermon preached at St. Saviour's Church,
Forest Hill.
By the Rev. M. Margoliouth, LL.D., Ph.D., etc.
Octavo .. .. | 0 1 0

Rules for Christian Conduct.
With Scripture Illustrations: being the Scripture
Ethics of St. Basil the Great.
Edited by John M. Maguire, B.A.
Foolscap octavo. Sewed .. .. | 0 1 0

Universal History.

CONTENTS :— The First Part contains :— 1. The
Antediluvian period. 2. The period from the Deluge
to the building of Babel. 3. From Nimrod to Saul.
4. From Saul to Nebuchadnezzar, or the times of
Israel's kings. 5. From Nebuchadnezzar to Cyrus, or
the first Gentile kingdom. 6. From Cyrus to Alexander,
or the second Gentile kingdom. 7. The times of Alexander, or the third Gentile kingdom. 8. The times of
the successors of Alexander, or the four divisions of the
third kingdom. 9. The times of the Maccabees, or the
temporary revival of the Jewish people. 10. The
Roman Commonwealth, or the fourth Gentile kingdom.

£ s. d.

The Second Part, includes the times of the Pagan
Roman Emperors, and the times of Constantine the
Great, with the history of the Church during the first
three centuries.

The Third Part, gives the history of the decline and
breaking up of the Pagan Roman Empire, and of the
establishment of false Christianity and Mahometanism.

The Fourth Part, contains the history of the
Western Roman Empire, broken into the modern
kingdoms of Europe; it embraces also the story of the
decline and fall of the Eastern Roman Empire, and
the deeds of the Turks, Tartars, etc.

The whole Work closes with a general recapitula-
tion of the World's History.

Seven Volumes, Foolscap octavo.   2   2   0

₊ Volumes VI. and VII., which include the His-
tory from the Reformation to the Accession of Queen
Victoria, may be obtained alone, price 0 10   6

The Greek Ecclesiastical Historians.

Eusebius; Evagrius; Theodoret; Socrates; Sozo-
men.
Six Volumes, Octavo, Cloth 1 10   0

Index to the Holy Scriptures.

CONTENTS:—Alphabetical Index, comprising the
Names, Characters, and Subjects, both of the Old and
New Testaments, 40 pp.

Octavo. Sewed   0   1   6

Ditto.
Foolscap octavo.   Sewed   ..   0   1   0

Ditto.
16mo.   Sewed   0   1   0

Ditto.
32mo.   Sewed   0   1   0

For Specimen Pages, see the Illustrated Supplement. By post, free.

	£	s.	d.

· **The Warrant of Faith.**

CONTENTS:—Preface, 10 *pp.* Chap. I. The Necessity and Reasonableness of a Revelation. Chap. II. The Bible an Authentic Revelation—the Formation of the Canon—the Canon of the Old Testament. Chap. III. The Apocryphal Additions and Critical Objections made to the Canon of the Old Testament. Chap. IV. The Canon of the New Testament. Chap. V. The Epistle to the Hebrews. Chap. VI. The Controverted Catholic Epistles. Chap. VII. The Revelation. Chap. VIII. The Bible the Word of God—its Witnesses. Chap. IX. The Bible Plenarily Inspired—its own Testimony. Chap. X. The Bible Plenarily Inspired: External Testimony. Chap. XI. Defective and Rationalistic Views of Inspiration. Chap. XII. Rationalistic Views of Inspiration—continued. Chap. XIII. The Difficulties of Scripture. Chap XIV. The Integrity, Intrinsic Excellence, and Authority of the Bible, 480 *pp.* By the Rev. Robert Whytehead, M.A.

Post octavo, Cloth .. .. | 0 | 6 | 6 |

Scriptural Coincidences.

CONTENTS: Preface, 2 *pp.* The Coincidences of Scripture, or Traits of Truth. 138 *pp.* By the Rev. J. Duncan Craig, D.D.

12mo, Cloth .. .. | 0 | 3 | 0 |

Sunday Afternoon.

CONTENTS:—A series of Pictures and Poems upon Old Testament History, with an ample collection of Questions to assist in the Study of Scripture. The Work contains 72 Plates, 113 Poems, and 3500 Scripture Questions.

Foolscap octavo, Extra cloth, gilt leaves .. .. | 0 | 8 | 6 |

The Apocrypha.

Quarto, Cloth .. | 0 | 4 | 0 |

Ditto.

Octavo, Cloth .. | 0 | 3 | 6 |

Ditto.

Foolscap octavo, Cloth .. .. | 0 | 2 | 0 |

For Specimen Pages, see the Illustrated Supplement. By post, free.

		£	s.	d.

Prolegomena in Biblia Polyglotta.
  By Professor Samuel Lee.
    Quarto, Cloth　.. 　　.. 　　　　　　　.. 　| 0 7 6 |

CVIII. Bible Pictorial Illustrations.
    With full descriptions from Scripture.
  By Charles Bell Birch.
    Foolscap octavo, Cloth .. 　　.. 　　.. 　　　.. 　| 0 12 0 |

The Jansenists.
    CONTENTS :—Their Rise, Persecution by the Jesuits,
    and existing Remnant. A Chapter in Church History,
    98 pp. With 4 Illustrations.
  By S. P. Tregelles, LL.D.
    Post octavo, Cloth 　　.. 　　.. 　　　　　.. 　| 0 3 6 |

The Bible of Every Land.
    CONTENTS :—A History of the Sacred Scriptures in
    every Language and Dialect into which Translations
    have been made. Illustrated by Specimen portions in
    Native Characters, Series of Alphabets, coloured Ethno-
    graphical Maps, Tables, Indexes, etc., 475 pp. "Our
    readers may form some idea of its contents when we
    tell them that there are here specimens of the Bible in
    about two hundred and twenty-five different languages
    and dialects, illustrated with maps, letterpress, and an
    important disquisition on the nature of the language,
    the history of the Translation, and the effects produced
    in a Missionary point of view. The Work is really, in
    the highest sense of the word, a History of the Bible,
    its spread, progress, and present condition. It is such a
    history, illustrated in the most graphic and artistic
    manner; and a wonderful history it is, as it is here
    brought before us, displaying an amount of labour,
    research, and skill, beside which all other books and
    works of man dwindle into utter insignificance."—
    Record.
    Quarto, Cloth 　.. 　.. 　.. 　.. 　.. 　.. 　| 0 10 6 |

For Specimen Pages, see the Illustrated Supplement. By post, free.

	£	s.	d.

Coverdale's English Bible.

CONTENTS:—Portrait of Bishop Coverdale. Preface, 2 pp. Memoir, 21 pp. Bibliographical Description, 4 pp. Facsimile Title-page. Coverdale's Address to King Henry the Eighth, 5 pp. The Prologue to the Christian Reader, 5 pp. The Old Testament, 816 pp. The Apocrypha, 187 pp. The New Testament, 268 pp.

	£	s.	d.
Crown quarto. Cloth	0	15	0
Turkey morocco plain	1	0	0
„ „ tooled	1	8	0
Antique morocco or russia	1	5	0

Ditto.

	£	s.	d.
Royal quarto, Cloth	1	1	0
Turkey morocco plain	1	10	0
„ „ tooled	4	0	0
Antique morocco or russia	5	0	0

Cruden's Concordance.

CONTENTS:—All the Words used through the Sacred Scriptures are Alphabetically arranged, with Reference to the various places where they occur.

Heretofore, Cruden's Concordance has been so bulky as to be necessarily confined to the bookcase or study, and is consequently seldom at hand when the memory demands assistance. With the hope of accommodating the Christian public with a portable Concordance for constant and convenient use, the larger edition is now presented in a very small volume. To secure the necessary condensation of the matter—1st, The "signification and explanation of words" has been dispensed with, as not requisite in a *Concordance;* and, 2udly, The words of the *Apocrypha* are omitted. The present edition contains, however, every appellative or common word, and every proper name, without omission, but gives no more than a reference to the passages. The whole Concordance is now also, for the first time, brought under one alphabet. This Concordance is uniform in size with the Polyglot Bibles, and has been printed to correspond with numerous other editions.

	£	s.	d.
Quarto, Cloth	0	6	0

For Specimen Pages, see the Illustrated Supplement. By post, free.

	£	s.	d.
Cruden's Concordance.			
Octavo, Cloth	0	4	6
Ditto.			
Foolscap octavo, Cloth ..	0	4	0
Ditto.			
32mo., Cloth	0	2	6
Cruden's Concordance to the New Testament.			
Foolscap	0	1	4
Ditto.			
32mo.	0	1	4

Authenticity of the Book of Daniel.

> CONTENTS :—A Defence of its Authenticity. 79 *pp.*
> By S. P. Tregelles, LL.D.

Foolscap octavo. Sewed ..	0	1	6

Daniel's Prophetic Visions.

> CONTENTS :—Preface, 12 *pp.* Coloured Map of the
> Ancient Persian and Roman Empires, with Description.
> Remarks on the Visions in the Book of Daniel, with
> Notes on Prophetic Interpretation in connection with
> Popery, and a Defence of the Authenticity of the Book
> of Daniel, 200 *pp.* Index, 6 *pp.*
> By S. P. Tregelles, LL.D.

Small octavo, Cloth	0	5	0

Divine Promises Illustrated.

> CONTENTS :— This is a Collection of the principal
> Divine Promises, Illustrated with appropriate passages
> of Scripture.

32mo., Roan	0	1	4

" It is Written."

> In an age when questions of every degree of interest
> are freely discussed, it is of the utmost importance to
> bring under general notice the demonstration of the
> Inspiration of the Scriptures in all their parts.
> CONTENTS :—The complete Inspiration of the Holy
> Scriptures—Scriptural Proof of Divine Inspiration—
> Examination of objections—Examination of evasions—
> Sacred criticism considered in its relation to Inspiration
> —Concluding observations, 104 *pp.*
> From the French of Professor Gaussen.

Post octavo, Cloth	0	5	0

For Specimen Pages, see the Illustrated Supplement. By post, free.

	£	s.	d.

The Names and Titles of our Lord Jesus Christ.

32mo., Cloth   ..   .. | 0 | 0 | 4

The Book of Proverbs, with References.

32mo., Roan   ..   .. | 0 | 0 | 6

The Hundred and Tenth Psalm.

CONTENTS:—Preface, 10 *pp.* A Translation from
the Hebrew of Psalm CX., with explanatory Notes,
20 *pp.*

Square 16mo., Cloth   .. | 0 | 1 | 4

Church Government.

CONTENTS:—A Discourse wherein the Rights of the
Church, and the Supremacy of Christian Princes, are
Vindicated and Adjusted, 419 *pp.*

By Archbishop Potter.

Octavo, Cloth   ..   .. | 0 | 5 | 0

Thesaurus Græcæ Linguæ:

CONSPECTUS eorum quæ in hac Thesauri Stephaniani
Editione continentur:—Henrici Stephani Admonitio de
Thesauri sui Epitome, quæ titulum Lexici Græco-Latini
Novi præfert. Epistola Dedicatoria, et Epigrammata
duo de Thesauro Gr. Catalogus Auctorum Græcorum,
e quorum Scriptis Vocabula et loquendi Genera, eorum
item unde Expositiones Vocabulorum aut loquendi
Generum petitæ sunt in hoc Thesauro Græcæ Linguæ.
Scipionis Carteromachi Pistoriensis Oratio de Laudibus
Literarum Græcarum. M. Antonii Antimachii de Li-
terarum Græcarum Laudibus Oratio. Conradi Heres-
bachii Oratio in Commendationem Græcarum Literarum.
H. Stephani ad Lectorem Epistola, seu Præfatio in suum
Thesaurum Linguæ Græcæ. Excerpta ex H. Stephani
Epistola, a 1559, edita, qua ad multas multorum Ami-
corum respondet, de suæ Typographiæ Statu, nominatim-
que de suo Thesauro Linguæ Græcæ. Excerpta ex
J. A. Fabricii Bibliotheca Græca: Lexica Græco-Latina
recentiorum. Excerpta ex Vita H. Stephani Secundi,
a Mic. Maittaire conscripta. De Verbis Græcorum
Mediis Commentationes L. Kusteri, J. Clerici, S. Clarkii,
et F. Schmidii, recensuit, auxit, suamque adjecit Chr.

For Specimen Pages, see the Illustrated Supplement. By post, free.

6

Wolle; cum Dresigii et Bowyeri Notis. P. P. M. ;
Ogerius de Linguæ Græcæ Affinitate cum Hebraica.
J. A. Ernesti de Vestigiis Linguæ Hebraicæ in Lingua
Græca Oratio.

LEXICON Vocum Peregrinarum in Scriptoribus
Græcis obviarum : in quo comprehenduntur:—Excerpta
e Chr. D. Beckii Dissertatione de Lexicis Græcis et
Latinis omnino, et recentissimis singulatim.   P. E.
Jablonskii Disquisitio de Lycaonica et aliis Linguis.
Fr. Guil. Sturzii de Dialecto Macedonica et Alexandrina
Liber. P. E. Jablonskii Glossarium Vocum Ægypti-
arum, cum J. Guil. Tewateri Auctario. L. C. Valckenærii
Dissertatio de Vocabulo Βάφις. Spicilegium Vocum
Ægyptiarum : post Jablonskium, Tewaterum, et Stur-
zium collegerunt Thesauri Stephaniani Editores. Ad-
denda et Corrigenda in Spicilegium Vocum Ægyptiarum.
J. G. Dahleri Lexicon Vocum Peregrinarum in Græcis
Auctoribus, Glossographis maxime, obviarum. Vocabula
a Dahlero prætermissa.

THESAURUS Linguæ Græcæ, ab H. Stephano con-
structus. Addenda huic Thesauro. Godofredi Hermanni
Dissertatio de Particula Άν. Index Thesauri novi
Stephaniani.

GLOSSARIA, et alia Opuscula:—Cyrilli, Philoxeni,
aliorumque Veterum Auctorum Glossaria, Græco-Latina
et Latino-Græca, a Carolo Labbæo collecta, plurimis in
locis ab Editoribus Thesauri Græci Stephaniani emen-
data. Bon. Vulcanii Brug. Notæ et Castigationes in
Glossaria utriusque Linguæ. Colloquia duo Vetera
Græco-Latina; Colloquium Scholasticum; Excerpta e
Verweii Præfatione ad Novam Viam Docendi Græca.
Niciarii Interrogationes et Responsiones; Carfilidis
Interrogationes et Responsa; Responsa Sapientum.
Præcepta in Delphis ab Apolline in Columna scripta
secus Deum. Collectio Vocum, quæ pro diversa Signifi-
catione Accentum diversum accipiunt, Auctore Cyrillo,
seu potius Philopono. Veteres Glossæ Verborum Juris,
quæ passim in Basilicis reperiuntur, a Carolo Labbæo
edita, cum Excerptis e Fabricii Bibliotheca Græca,
Antonii Schultingii Præfatione, Additionibus e Libro
Mr., Jos. Scaligeri et aliorum Emendationibus, et Notis
ejusdem Ant. Schultingii. Hadriani Sententiæ, Responsa, Rescripta, et Epistolæ, cum Excerptis de Dositheo
e Fabricii Bibliotheca Græca, et cum Goldasti Notis.
Verborum quorundam Themata, quæ magna e parte vel
sunt Anomala, vel Poetica, aut certe ejusmodi, ut non
obviam cuilibet habeant Originem. De Græcæ Linguæ
Dialectis, e Scriptis Joannis Grammatici, quæ Τεχνικά
fuerunt inscripta; De Dialectis a Corintho decerpta ;

F. Plutarcho Excerpta de Dialectis, et Homerico earum
Usu; Ex eodem Plutarcho Excerpta de Tropis, et
Homerico earum Usu; De Schematis, et Homerico
eorum Usu, ex eodem Plutarcho. De Passionibus
Dictionum, e Tryphone Grammatico; Ejusdem Opuscula
quædam, e Museo Critico Cantabrigiensi, cum Notis
C. J. Blomfieldii, Episcopi olim Cestrensis, nunc Lon-
dinensis, excerpta e Fabricii Bibliotheca Græca.
Herodiani de Notis Numerorum Tractatus. De Men-
suris et Ponderibus, Libellus Galeni, e Collatione eum
iis, quæ apud Paulum Ægin. et Schol. Nicandri leguntur,
emendatus. De Mensibus et Partibus eorundem, cum
Excerptis e Matthæi Glossariis Græcis Minoribus. Am-
monii de Similibus et Differentibus Vocabulis Libellus,
cum Excerptis e Fabricii Bibliotheca Græca, Valckenærii
Præfatione, Notis, et Animadversionibus integris; Nova
Editio correctior, et Notis e Schæferi editione Lipsi-
ensi A.D. 1822, atque ea, quam continet Scapulæ Lexicon
Oxoniense A.D. 1820, depromtis aucta. Cui accesserunt
e Valckenærii editione Opuscula Eranii Philonis de
Differentia Significationis, Lesbonactis de Figuris Gram-
maticis, Anonymi de Solœcismo et Barbarismo, Lexicon
de Spiritibus Dictionum, e Tryphone, Chœrobosco,
Theodorito, et aliis collectum, cum Notis e Schæferi
editione atque Oxoniensi Scapulæ Lexici editione
de,umtis. Τάξις Παλαιὰ καὶ Ὀνομασίαι τῶν Ἀρχόντων,
secundum H. Stephani Editionem. Kusterianum Suidam,
et Montefalconii Bibliothecam Coislinianam, e qua
desumta sunt Ὀνόματα τῶν Ἀρμάτων. Orbicii Περὶ τῶν
περὶ τὸ Στράτευμα Τάξεων. H. Stephani Commentarius
de Atticæ Linguæ seu Dialecti Idiomatis.

Ab Henrico Stephano constructus.

Eight volumes Folio. Half-russia, marbled leaves . | 10 0 0

Sixteen volumes Folio, Half-cloth, marbled leaves.. | 8 0 0

Hayter on Perspective and Drawing.

CONTENTS:—An Introduction to Perspective, Practical Geometry, Drawing and Painting; in a series of
familiar Dialogues between the Author's children, and
letters addressed to his pupils. Illustrated with numerous
Wood Engravings, from Drawings by John Hayter, Esq.

By Charles Hayter, Esq.

Octavo, Cloth .. .. | 0 5 0

For Specimen Pages, see the Illustrated Supplement. By post, free.

	£	s.	d.
Bunyan's Pilgrim's Progress.			
With Illustrations.			
Foolscap octavo, Cloth	0	1	0
Ditto.			
Octavo, Cloth	0	2	0
Bunyan's Pilgrim's Progress, in Verse.			
Foolscap octavo, Cloth	0	1	0
Bunyan's Life.			
Foolscap octavo, Cloth	0	1	0
Mamma's Absence : A Tale.			
Square, Cloth	0	0	6
The Robin of Woodside Lodge.			
A true Story. With Illustrations.			
Square, Cloth	0	1	0
The Way of Faith.			
CONTENTS :—Prefaces, 12 *pp.* Chronological Table, 2 *pp.* Selections from all the Books of Holy Writ, for the use of Jewish Schools and Families, under the sanction of the Chief Rabbi of the United Congregations of the British Empire, 374 *pp.*			
By Dr. M. Büdinger.			
Octavo, Cloth	0	4	0
The Psalms, with Scripture Illustrations.			
CONTENTS :—The Book of Psalms, illustrated with suitable Scripture passages.			
32mo., Roan	0	2	6

For Specimen Pages, see the Illustrated Supplement. By post, free.

	£	s.	d.

The Proverbs, with Scripture Illustrations.

> CONTENTS:—The Book of Proverbs, illustrated with suitable Scripture passages.
> 32mo., Roan 0 1 8

St. John's Gospel, with Scripture Illustrations.

> CONTENTS:—St. John's Gospel, illustrated with suitable Scripture passages.
> 32mo., Roan 0 1 8

Hebrews, with Scripture Illustrations.

> CONTENTS:—The Epistle to the Hebrews, illustrated with suitable Scripture passages.
> 32mo., Roan 0 1 4

Romans, with Scripture Illustrations.

> CONTENTS:—The Epistle to the Romans, illustrated with suitable Scripture passages.
> 32mo., Roan 0 1 4

A Brief Reply to " Essays and Reviews."

> By Henry Craik.
> Octavo. Sewed 0 0 4

Revision of our English Bible.

> CONTENTS:—Preface. 2 pp. Hints and Suggestions on the Revision of our English Bible, 60 pp.
> By Henry Craik.
> Foolscap octavo. Sewed 0 0 6

Characteristics of the Languages of Asia and Europe.

> This Work is designed to furnish an Elementary Introduction to the Comparative Study of Languages, 60 pp.
> By Henry Craik.
> Crown octavo. Sewed 0 1 0

The Pentateuchal Narrative Vindicated

> From the absurdities charged against it by the Bishop of Natal, 22 pp.
> By John Collyer Knight.
> Octavo. Sewed 0 0 8

For Spurious Pages, see the Illustrated Supplement. By post, free.

£ s. d.

Scripture Helps for Confirmation.

> CONTENTS:—Suggestive thoughts for the day. Answers to enquiry for direction. Encouragements under conscious weakness. Directions for future life. Prayers for Divine help. Sponsor's thought. The Sponsor's desire and Prayers. Text for every day in the Week, 12 pp.
>
> Royal 32mo. Sewed 0 0 3

The Roman Census.

> CONTENTS:—An Explanation of Luke ii. 1-5, with reference to the Birth-day of our Lord, established on independent historical grounds, 16 pp.
>
> By Johannes von Gumpach.
>
> Octavo. Sewed 0 0 8

The Incredibilities of the Pentateuch. Part II.

> CONTENTS:—Remarks on the Bishop of Natal's Work upon the Pentateuch, 20 pp.
>
> By John Collyer Knight.
>
> Octavo. Sewed 0 0 9

Scriptural Predestination.

> CONTENTS:—Preface, 2 pp. Introduction, 10 pp. Paraphrase on St. Paul's Epistle to the Ephesians, 16 pp. The Doctrine of Scriptural Predestination briefly stated and considered. With some remarks on the Baptismal Question, 67 pp.
>
> By the Rev. Robert Knight.
>
> Octavo, Cloth 0 5 0

The Plurality of Worlds.

> CONTENTS:— Introduction, 12 pp. The Positive argument from Scripture; with answers to some late objections from analogy, 141 pp.
>
> By the Rev. Robert Knight.
>
> Crown octavo, Cloth 0 5 6

• **St. Matthew's Gospel.**

> CONTENTS:—Preface, 2 pp. Introduction, 4 pp. A New Translation, with brief Notes, and a Harmony of the Four Gospels, 205 pp.
>
> By John H. Godwin.
>
> Crown octavo, Cloth 0 5 0

For Specimen Pages, see the Illustrated Supplement. By post, free.

	£ s. d.

The Physical History of the Earth.

> CONTENTS:—Facts our guide; the Mosaic Record a fact; Division of the History; the Pre-historical Period; the Azoic Era: Succession and Division of Strata; the Geological Theory; the Systems of Rocks; the Protozoic Era; the Mesozoic Era; Genesis; Evidences of Sudden Change; the First Day; the Results of Rotation; the Second Day; the Third Day; the Fourth Day; the Fifth Day; the Sixth Day; the Antediluvian Period; the Deluge: Drying up of the Waters; Change in the Earth's Axis; the Glacial Epoch; Antiquity of Man; the Post-diluvian Period; Results; Conclusion, 134 pp.
>
> 12mo., Cloth 0 3 6

The Sixty-eighth Psalm.

> CONTENTS:—Preface. 6 pp. Psalm lxviii. Translated from the Hebrew. With Explanatory Notes, 47 pp.
>
> Square 16mo., Cloth 0 1 6

The Second Psalm.

> CONTENTS:—Preface, 3 pp. A Translation from the Hebrew of Psalm ii., with Explanatory Notes, 12 pp.
>
> Square 16mo., Cloth 0 1 4

Christ on the Cross.

> CONTENTS:—Introductory Epistle, 17 pp. An Exposition of the Twenty-second Psalm, 426 pp.
>
> By the Rev. John Stevenson, D.D., Hon. Canon of Canterbury.
>
> Post octavo, Cloth 0 5 0

The Lord our Shepherd.

> CONTENTS:— An Exposition of the Twenty-third Psalm, 297 pp.
>
> By the Rev. John Stevenson, D.D., Hon. Canon of Canterbury.
>
> Post octavo, Cloth 0 3 6

Gratitude.

> An Exposition of the Hundred and third Psalm.
>
> CONTENTS:—I. Call to Personal Gratitude. II. The Pardon of Sin. III. The Healing of Disease. IV. The Life Redeemed from Destruction. V. The Crown of Loving-kindness and Tender Mercies. VI. The Mouth

satisfied with Good, and the Strength Renewed. VII. The Lord executing Judgment for the Oppressed. VIII. The Lord making known His ways to Men. IX. Manifold Benefits flowing out of the Character of God through Christ. X. Immeasurable Benefits—Mercy. XI. Immeasurable Benefits—Forgiveness. XII. Immeasurable Benefits—Pity. XIII. Everlasting Benefits —Mercy. XIV. Everlasting Benefits—Righteousness. XV. The Everlasting and Prepared Throne. XVI. The Everlasting and Universal Kingdom.—Call to Universal Gratitude. XVII. Angels. XVIII. All the Hosts of the Lord. XIX. All the Works of the Lord. XX. The Psalmist's own Soul, 356 *pp.*

By the Rev. John Stevenson, D.D., Hon. Canon of Canterbury.

Post octavo, Cloth .. 0 3 6

Sanctification through the Truth.

By the Rev. John Stevenson, D.D., Hon. Canon of Canterbury.

Crown octavo, Cloth 0 1 0

ditto   Sewed 0 0 6

The Second Advent.

Contents:—A Letter to the Author, from Dr. Marsh; Suggestions for Scripture Study of the Second Advent, 42 *pp.*

By the Rev. John Stevenson, D.D., Hon. Canon of Canterbury.

Crown octavo, Cloth 0 1 0

Perfect Love.

Contents:—Introduction, 10 *pp.* Memorials of John and Elizabeth Wolfe; with an Appendix, 202 *pp.*

By the Rev. John Stevenson, D.D., Hon. Canon of Canterbury.

Foolscap octavo, Cloth 0 1 0

For Specimen Pages, see the Illustrated Supplement. By post, free.

£ s. d.

Tenfold Blessings be yours.

A Letter to a Friend, 8 pp.

By the Rev. John Stevenson. D.D., Hon. Canon of Canterbury.
32mo. Sewed. Price, per 100 .. .. .. | 0 3 0

Happy and Blessed is the True Believer.

Extracted from "The Lord our Shepherd," an Exposition of Psalm xxiii.

By the Rev. John Stevenson, D.D., Hon. Canon of Canterbury.
32mo. Sewed. Price, per 100 .. .. .. 0 3 0

The Scriptures Arranged

By the Rev. H. P. Linton, M.A.
Foolscap octavo., Cloth 0 6 0

The Psalms of David and Solomon.

By the Rev. H. P. Linton, M.A.
Foolscap octavo 0 3 0

Christ in the Old Testament;

Or, the Footsteps of the Redeemer, as revealed in Type, in Prophecy, in Sacrifice, and in Personal Manifestation, from the Creation to His birth.

By the Rev. H. P. Linton, M.A.
Foolscap octavo, Cloth .. .. .. | 0 5 0

Sketches and Scenes from the Life of David.

By the Rev. H. P. Linton, M.A.
18mo. Sewed 0 0 6

Imputed Righteousness.

By the Rev. H. P. Linton, M.A.
18mo. Sewed 0 0 3

Monthly Union Volumes.

By the Rev. H. P. Linton, M.A.

A Chart of Ancient History.

By the Rev. H. P. Linton, M.A.
Intended to Illustrate Prophecy.
Coloured .. .. | 0 3 0

For Specimen Pages, see the Illustrated Supplement. By post, free.

	£	s.	d.

A Chart of Modern History.

Giving the rise of the European Kingdoms.
By the Rev. H. P. Linton, M.A.

Coloured .. .. | 0 | 1 | 0 |

**Monthly Union Paper, for simultaneous Reading and
Prayer** .. .. | 0 | 0 | 0½ |

By the Rev. H. P. Linton, M.A.

The Apostolic Canons.

CONTENTS:—Preface, 2 pp. The Canons in Greek,
Latin, and English, with Notes. 30 pp.
By the Rev. Thomas MacNally, A.M., LL.B.

Octavo. Sewed .. .. | 0 | 1 | 0 |

The Gospels Consolidated.

The object of this compilation has been to consolidate
the matter of the four Gospels so as to form it into one
continuous narrative, and at the same time to enable the
reader to ascertain with facility the source from which
each part has been derived. The main endeavour has
been, by placing the Gospel narrative before the reader
in the form in which other narratives are now usually
written, to enable him, unconsciously as it were, to re-
ceive all the information furnished by the four Gospels
combined, without the labour and distraction of consulting
the several Gospels; and, at the same time, to facilitate
reference to the Gospels themselves for verification of
the text.

A full Index to the Gospel History is also appended.
102 pp.

Quarto, Cloth .. .. | 0 | 6 | 0 |

The Expressive Reading of the Sacred Scriptures, as
promoted by Emphasised Translation, according to the
logical Idiom of the Original Greek.

CONTENTS:—I. Importance of Reading the Bible
Well. II. Expository Value of Emphasis. III. Autho-
ritative Indication of Emphasis. IV. Law of Emphasis
Explained. V. Proof of an Emphatic Idiom. VI. Em-
phasised Translation Needed. VII. Plan of a Proposed
Emphasised Translation, 32 pp.
By Joseph B. Rotherham.

Octavo. Sewed .. .. | 0 | 0 | 6 |

For Specimen Pages, see the Illustrated Supplement. By post, free.

	£	s.	d.

A Key to the Pentateuch.
Foolscap octavo. Sewed .. | 0 | 0 | 6

Comments on the Epistle of James.
By Robert Nelson.
Crown octavo, Cloth .. .. | 0 | 1 | 6

Comments on the Epistle to the Hebrews.
By Robert Nelson.
Crown octavo, Cloth .. .. | 0 | 6 | 0

Narratives from the Old Testament;
in Familiar Language. For the use of the Young.
Cloth .. .. | 0 | 1 | 6

Studies on the Complutensian Polyglot.
By the Professor Delitzsch.
Price .. .. | 0 | 1 | 6

St. Peter's Commentary on the 119th Psalm.
Foolscap octavo .. .. | 0 | 0 | 6

The Original Language of St. Matthew's Gospel;
with particular reference to Dr. Davidson's Introduction
to the New Testament.
By S. P. Tregelles, LL.D.
Octavo. Sewed .. .. .. | 0 | 0 | 6

A Greek Lesson Card.
Containing the Greek Alphabet, with Examples; an
interlinear Greek and English Exercise, and explanatory
Remarks.
Price .. .. | 0 | 0 | 3

The Invalid's Hymn Book.
By the Rev. Hugh White.
Cloth .. .. | 0 | 1 | 6

Chaldee Paradigms.
Being the Chaldee Portion of the Grammatical Introduction to the Analytical Hebrew and Chaldee Lexicon.
Quarto. Sewed .. .. | 0 | 2 | 6

The Pentateuch according to the Talmud.
Parts I.—II.—III.—and IV.
Compiled by P. I. Hershon.
Each Part .. .. | 0 | 1 | 6

For Specimen Pages, see the Illustrated Supplement. By post, free.

Harmony of Prophecies on the Restoration of Israel and Judah.   £ s. d.

> CONTENTS:—I. The Gathering; II. The Tribulation; III. The Repentance; IV. The Sanctification; V. The Prosperity; VI. The Rejoicing; VII. The House of David; VIII. The Temple; IX. The Glory of God; X. The Holy Waters; XI. The Ordinances for the Prince; XII. The Ordinances for the Priests; XIII. The Boundaries and Allotments.
>
> By M. D. C. WALTERS, M.A., a Senior Chaplain H.M. Bengal Establishment.
>
> Crown octavo 0 1 6

Tyndale's New Testament published in 1526.

> Being the first Translation from Greek into English. Reprinted Verbatim; with a Memoir of his Life and Writings. Together with the proceedings and correspondence of Henry VIII., Sir T. More, and Lord Cromwell.
>
> By George Offor.
>
> Octavo 0 10 0
>
> *⁎* A few large-paper copies illuminated.

Arabic Ritual.

> 12mo., Cloth 0 1 6

The Family Worship Book :

> Being Scripture Portions; arranged for Family Reading throughout the year.
>
> In Twelve Monthly Parts, stiff wrapper, commencing January 1, 1874.
>
> Quarto..   ..   .. each   0 1 0
> Four Quarterly Parts   ..   ..   .. each   0 6 0
>
> An elegant Cloth Case to be given with the last Part to each Subscriber.

Thoughts on the Book of Job :

> By R. E. Hutchinson, Esq., M.D., M.R.C.S.E., Surgeon-Major, Bengal Army. *In the Press.*

Records of the Past :

> Being English Translations of the Assyrian and Egyptian Monuments. Published under the sanction of the Society of Biblical Archæology.
>
> CONTENTS OF VOL. I.—1. Inscription of Rimmon Nirari, by the Rev. A. H. Sayce, M.A.; 2. Inscription of Khammurabi, by H. Fox Talbot, F.R.S., etc.; 3. Monolith Inscription of Samas-Himmon, by the Rev. A. H. Sayce, M.A.; 4. Bellino's Cylinder of Sennacherib, by H. Fox Talbot, F.R.S., etc.; 5. Taylor's Cylinder of Sennacherib, by H. Fox Talbot, F.R.S., etc.;

6. Annals of Assurbanipal, by George Smith; 7. Behistun Inscription of Darius, by Sir H. Rawlinson, K.C.B., D.C.L. ; 8. Babylonian Exorcisms, by the Rev. A. H. Sayce, M.A.; 9. Table of Assyrian Weights and Measures, by the Rev. A. H. Sayce, M.A. 10. Legend of Ishtar, by H. Fox Talbot, F.R.S., etc.; 11. Early Astronomical Tablets, by the Rev. A. H. Sayce, M.A.; 12. Assyrian Calendar, by the Rev. A. H. Sayce, M.A.; List of further Texts, Assyrian and Egyptian, selected by Geo. Smith, and P. Le Page Renouf, F.R.S.L.

	£	s.	d.
Cloth	0	3	6

WORKS by the Rev. JOHN STEVENSON, D.D.

Hon. Canon of Canterbury.

	£	s.	d.
Christ on the Cross.			
Post octavo, Cloth ..	0	5	0
The Lord our Shepherd.			
An Exposition of the Twenty-third Psalm.			
Post octavo, Cloth	0	3	6
Gratitude.			
An Exposition of the Hundred and third Psalm.			
Post octavo, Cloth	0	3	6
Sanctification through the Truth.			
Crown octavo, Cloth	0	1	0
ditta. Sewed	0	0	6
The Second Advent.			
Crown octavo, Cloth	0	1	0
Perfect Love.			
Foolscap octavo, Cloth	0	1	0
Tenfold Blessings be Yours.			
32mo. Sewed. Per 100	0	3	0
Happy and Blessed is the True Believer.			
Extracted from " The Lord our Shepherd," an Exposition of Psalm xxiii.			
32mo. Sewed. Per 100	0	3	0

For Specimen Pages, see the Illustrated Supplement. By post, free.

WORKS by the Rev. H. P. LINTON, M.A.,
St. Paul's Vicarage, Birkenhead.

	£	s.	d.
The Scriptures Arranged.			
Foolscap octavo, Cloth ..	0	6	0
The Psalms of David and Solomon.			
Foolscap octavo ..	0	3	0
Christ in the Old Testament ;			
Or, the Footsteps of the Redeemer, as revealed in Type, in Prophecy, in Sacrifice, and in Personal Manifestation, from the Creation to His birth.			
Foolscap octavo, Cloth ..	0	3	0
Sketches and Scenes in the Life of David.			
18mo. Sewed. ..	0	0	6
Imputed Righteousness.			
18mo. Sewed. ..	0	0	3
Monthly Union Volumes.			
A Chart of Ancient History.			
Intended to Illustrate Prophecy.			
Coloured ..	0	3	0
A Chart of Modern History.			
Giving the rise of the European Kingdoms.			
Coloured ..	0	3	0
Monthly Union Paper, for simultaneous Reading and Prayer ..	0	0	0½

WORKS by H. N. CHAMPNEY, Esq.,

	£	s.	d.
Short Family Prayers	0	1	0
Textual Commentary on the Psalms	0	3	0
Texts, for Family Worship, etc. ..	0	0	6
Index to the Liturgy ..	0	0	6
Churchman's Almanack	0	0	1
Handbills, for distribution (per 50)	0	0	6
Family Prayers for a Month	0	1	0
Clerical Reading and Bible Exterior Index ..	0	1	0
Heart Melodies ..	0	0	6

For *Specimen Pages, see the Illustrated Supplement. By post, free.*

www.ingramcontent.com/pod-product-compliance
Lightning Source LLC
Chambersburg PA
CBHW031440270326
41930CB00007B/807